Better Homes and Gardens®

LOW-WATTAGE MICROWAVE
COOKING

Our seal assures you that every recipe in
Low-Wattage Microwave Cooking
has been tested in the Better Homes and Gardens® Test Kitchen.
This means that each recipe is practical and reliable, and
meets our high standards of taste appeal.

BETTER HOMES AND GARDENS® BOOKS
Editor: Gerald M. Knox
Art Director: Ernest Shelton
Managing Editor: David A. Kirchner
Editorial Project Managers: James D. Blume, Marsha Jahns,
  Rosanne Weber Mattson

Department Head, Cook Books: Sharyl Heiken
Associate Department Heads: Sandra Granseth,
  Rosemary C. Hutchinson, Elizabeth Woolever
Senior Food Editors: Linda Henry, Marcia Stanley, Joyce Trollope
Associate Food Editors: Jennifer Darling, Mary Major,
  Diana McMillen, Mary Jo Plutt, Linda Foley Woodrum
Test Kitchen: Director, Sharon Stilwell; Photo Studio Director,
  Janet Herwig; Home Economists: Jean Brekke, Kay Cargill,
  Marilyn Cornelius, Maryellyn Krantz, Lynelle Munn,
  Dianna Nolin, Marge Steenson

Associate Art Directors: Neoma Thomas, Linda Ford Vermie,
  Randall Yontz
Assistant Art Directors: Lynda Haupert, Harijs Priekulis,
  Tom Wegner
Graphic Designers: Mary Schlueter Bendgen, Mike Burns,
  Brian Wignall
Art Production: Director, John Berg; Associate, Joe Heuer;
  Office Manager, Michaela Lester

President, Book Group: Jeramy Lanigan
Vice President, Retail Marketing: Jamie L. Martin
Vice President, Administrative Services: Rick Rundall

BETTER HOMES AND GARDENS® MAGAZINE
President, Magazine Group: James A. Autry
Editorial Director: Doris Eby
Editorial Services Director: Duane L. Gregg
Food and Nutrition Editor: Nancy Byal

MEREDITH CORPORATION OFFICERS
Chairman of the Executive Committee: E. T. Meredith III
Chairman of the Board: Robert A. Burnett
President: Jack D. Rehm

LOW-WATTAGE MICROWAVE COOKING
Editor: Mary Jo Plutt
Editorial Project Manager: Rosanne Weber Mattson
Graphic Designer: Mary Schlueter Bendgen
Electronic Text Processors: Kathy Benz, Joyce Wasson
Food Stylists: Jennifer Darling, Janet Herwig
Contributing Photographers: Mike Dieter, Scott Little
Contributing Illustrator: Thomas Rosborough

On the front cover: Creamy Shrimp Bisque
(see recipe, page 32)

In my research I've found that compact, 400- to 550-watt microwave ovens are among the best-selling kitchen appliances. Why? Because they're inexpensive, they don't take up much space, and they're lightweight and easy to move.

They do have one "catch," however—most microwave recipes are written for high-wattage (600- to 700-watt) ovens and often won't work successfully in low-wattage ovens.

But don't worry, the catch of owning a low-wattage oven is no longer a problem. As we tested this book, we found the *biggest* cooking difference between high- and low-wattage ovens is speed. Low-wattage ovens take a little longer to cook most foods. Also, because of their small cavities, they work best with smaller amounts of food. So, as we developed each recipe in this book, we made sure to keep those two important factors in mind. The result is micro-cooking made easier for you—no more guessing at cooking times or ingredient amounts.

Besides finding a heaping helping of kitchen-tested, *reliable* recipes in this book, you'll also discover plenty of low-wattage micro-cooking timings for heating, defrosting, and cooking convenience foods.

Now with *Low-Wattage Microwave Cooking* at your side, you'll be able to make the most of your low-wattage oven.

Mary Jo Plutt

Brush Up on Basics 6

Take the mystery out of microwave cooking by learning a few simple techniques.

Fast-Fixin' Beverages & Snacks 9

Counter a hunger attack with a made-in-a-minute beverage or snack.

Easy Main Dishes 17

No time to cook? No problem. Just mix, zap, and serve one of these tasty main dishes.

Brush Up On Basics

What's the difference between cooking in a low-wattage oven and in a high-wattage oven? Read below and we'll tell you.

We've included everything you'll need to know to take the guesswork out of using your compact oven.

Also, check the how-to photos on pages 48–51 and 64–75 for extra tips when cooking in your microwave oven.

What's What In Wattage

The largest difference among microwave ovens is the amount of cooking power they generate. The higher the wattage, the faster foods will cook on HIGH power.

Finding The Watts

If you're unsure what the wattage of your oven is, look first in your owner's manual, or check the label on your oven's back or door near the Underwriters Laboratories seal.

If you still can't find it, try this simple test: Heat 1 cup warm tap water (about 70°) in a 2-cup measure on HIGH (100% power). If the water boils in less than 3 minutes, your oven probably has 600 watts or more of output power. If it takes *longer* than 3 minutes, your oven probably has *less than* 600 watts of output cooking power.

Most microwave cook books are written for 600- to 700-watt ovens. This cook book was *specially* written and tested for compact, 400- to 550-watt ovens.

Power Peaks

In order for the recipe timings in this book to work, you'll need to make sure you're getting the maximum power from your microwave oven. How? Plug it into an outlet on a separate circuit from your other electrical appliances.

Is It Done Yet?

The recipe and chart timings in this book usually include a range of cooking times because microwave ovens will vary slightly from manufacturer to manufacturer.

To avoid overcooking foods, check the doneness of the food at the *minimum* recommended cooking time, then check after every 30 to 60 seconds.

If your oven doesn't have second increments,

check your watch or use a digital timer when cooking some recipes. Or, just count one thousand one, one thousand two. . . .

Also, don't use an extension cord on your microwave oven.

If you notice that your oven cooks slower at certain times of the day, you may be operating it during a peak power-usage period—when the outlet can't feed maximum power into the oven. During these times, you'll need to cook foods slightly longer. This is why in each recipe, along with the cooking times, we've included a description of what the food should look like when it's done.

Low-Wattage Oven Basics

Using Power Levels
Because most of the low-wattage ovens have either one or two power settings, the recipes and charts in this book cook using either HIGH (100% power) or DEFROST settings. If your oven has several power settings (such as 10%, 30%, 50%, 70%, and 100%), check your owner's manual for guidelines when selecting a lower power setting to defrost.

Selecting Microwave Cookware
One advantage of using a microwave oven is that you can mix, cook, and serve many foods in the same container. But be sure that you use only microwave-safe cookware for cooking in your oven. (See tip, page 8.)

Also, choosing the right shape of dish will help foods cook more evenly. Round dishes are best because the corners of square or rectangular dishes receive a double dose of microwaves, causing overcooking.

Most low-wattage microwave ovens have small cavities, so you'll need to use smaller cookware.

Before starting to cook a recipe, check to see that your dish fits in your oven. If you're using a turntable, make sure the dish won't hit the oven walls as it turns.

Handy cookware to use in compact microwave ovens includes: large mugs; medium-size dinner plates; cereal bowls; 7- and 9-inch pie plates; microwave-safe muffin pans; 1- and 1½-quart casseroles; individual-size cas-seroles; 1-, 2-, and 4-cup glass measuring cups; 6- and 10-ounce custard cups; 8x1½-inch round baking dishes; and microwave-safe bacon racks.

Also, keep microwave-safe paper towels and plastic wrap, plus waxed paper, on hand for convenient microwave covers. (See tip, page 18.)

Test It First

What's "micro-wave-safe" cookware? Many manufacturers will indicate whether their product is safe for microwave cooking. But if you can't find the information on your glass, pottery, or china container, then test it yourself. Here's how:

Pour ½ cup warm tap water (about 70°) into a 1-cup glass measure. Set it in the oven, beside the dish you're testing.

Micro-cook on HIGH for 1 minute. If the dish remains cool, you may use the dish for microwave cooking. If the dish is lukewarm, you may use the dish for heating food. If the dish is hot, *do not* use it in the microwave oven.

This test won't work for plastic containers because microwaves pass right through most plastics. To tell if a plastic container is microwave safe, you'll have to rely on the manufacturer's label.

Avoiding Hot Spots

Because microwaves fall randomly in the oven, some areas in your oven will be bombarded by more microwaves than others. Food in these "hot spots" cooks faster.

If you consistently see food in one area in your oven cooking faster than the rest, you probably have a hot spot in that area. (The edges of food, though, will always cook before its center.) If possible, avoid placing food in these areas in your oven when you can.

If you can't avoid these areas, then to keep foods cooking evenly you'll need to move the food around during cooking.

For example, by stirring or rearranging the food, you'll move the portion near the edges of the dish to the center. By rotating the dish, you'll be changing the location of the food in the oven.

Stirring the Foods

Rotating the Dish

Cleaning Your Oven

Food spatters in your oven divert the microwaves from the food you're cooking and add to the cooking time.

To keep your micro-wave oven clean, wipe out the inside right after cooking. For dried-on spatters, boil some water in a large measuring cup or bowl for a few minutes in the oven. The steam will soften the dried food.

Fast-Fixin' Beverages & Snacks

Whether you need a speedy pick-me-up to tide you over till dinner, or easy nibbles for a last-minute gathering, this chapter has a bundle of quick-to-make beverages and snacks for any occasion.

Keeping 'em Hot

With a touch of a button or a turn of a dial, you can use your microwave to reheat beverages and snacks in seconds.

Return the beverage or snack to the microwave oven and reheat on HIGH, checking after every 30 seconds and stirring or rearranging as necessary.

Remember, though, snacks made with tortillas and breads will get chewy and hard when reheated in the microwave, so our Test Kitchen recommends not reheating these.

A Popping Success

Microwave popcorn! Easy, fast, delicious, and no dirty dishes—you couldn't ask for a better snack food.

For best results in your low-wattage oven, follow these microwave-popcorn pointers:

● **Check your owner's manual:** Some microwave ovens are *not* recommended for popping popcorn.

● **Read *all* instructions on popcorn box/bag:** Since each brand of microwave popcorn is slightly different, popcorn manufacturers will include lots of information and tips on the package for using their product.

● **Use maximum power for maximum volume:** Popping popcorn uses lots of energy. So make sure your oven is operating on maximum power. Don't use an extension cord with your microwave oven and don't plug any other appliances into the same outlet. Also, keep the oven cavity clean. (See Power Peaks and Cleaning your Oven, pages 6 and 8.)

● **Experiment with different brands:** Try both the shelf-stable and frozen kinds of popcorn. Even though it's normal for a few unpopped kernels to remain in a fully popped bag, some brands of popcorn might pop better in your oven than other brands.

You might also want to try thawing frozen popcorn in the refrigerator for 2 hours before popping it— thawed popcorn requires less energy from your oven to pop it.

● **Prevent burning and scorching:** Popping popcorn in the microwave oven is easy and safe if you follow these few simple rules— don't repop unpopped kernels, use the bag only once, and don't leave the microwave oven unattended while popping the popcorn.

Also, *carefully* open the hot bag to avoid being burned by the steam.

Hot Buttered Rum

On a chilly evening, curl up with either the plain or apple-flavored version of this drink.

½ cup water
1 tablespoon brown sugar
2 teaspoons butter *or* margarine
2½ inches stick cinnamon *or* dash ground cinnamon
2 whole allspice *or* dash ground allspice
1½ ounces (3 tablespoons) rum

● In an 8- to 10-ounce mug combine water, brown sugar, butter, cinnamon, and allspice. Cook, uncovered, on HIGH for 2 to 3 minutes or till boiling. Then let stand for 5 minutes. Remove whole allspice. Stir in rum. Makes 1 (4-ounce) serving.

Hot Buttered Cider: Prepare Hot Buttered Rum as above, *except* substitute ½ cup *apple cider or apple juice* for the water.

Cranberry Sipper

Cranberry drink, apple, raisins, and spices combine for a simply super sipper!

1 tablespoon raisins
1 tablespoon rum (optional)
1 apple wedge
2½ to 3 inches stick cinnamon
Dash ground cloves
¾ cup cranberry-raspberry *or* cranberry-apple drink

● In an 8- to 10-ounce mug combine raisins, rum (if desired), apple wedge, cinnamon stick, and cloves. Then stir in cranberry drink. Cook, uncovered, on HIGH for 2 to 4 minutes or till hot and steamy. Makes 1 (6-ounce) serving.

Sugar- and Nut-Glazed Brie

A delicious contrast of sweet and savory flavors. (Pictured on page 13.)

Apple wedges, seedless grapes, assorted crackers, *or* a combination
Lemon juice
2 tablespoons brown sugar
2 tablespoons chopped walnuts, pecans, macadamia nuts, almonds, *or* hazelnuts (filberts)
1 teaspoon whiskey *or* brandy
1 4½- to 5-ounce round Brie cheese (about 3 inches in diameter)

● If serving apple wedges, brush them with lemon juice, then set them aside.

● In a 1-cup measure stir together brown sugar, nuts, and whiskey or brandy. Cook, uncovered, on HIGH for 30 seconds to 1 minute or till sugar is melted.

● Do not remove rind from cheese. Place cheese on a medium-size dinner plate. Spoon sugar mixture over cheese. Then cook, uncovered, on HIGH for 1 to 2 minutes or till the cheese is heated through but not melted.

● To serve, arrange apple wedges, grapes, or crackers around cheese. Makes 4 to 6 servings.

Maple-Glazed Sausage Links

Unexpected guests? Don't fret. Serve this quick, off-the-shelf appetizer.

2 tablespoons maple-flavored syrup
2 tablespoons catsup
½ teaspoon dry mustard
Dash ground ginger
1 5½-ounce package small smoked sausage links (2-inch links) *or* cocktail wieners

● For glaze, in a 1-quart casserole or bowl stir together syrup, catsup, mustard, and ginger.

● Stir in sausage links or wieners. Then cook, uncovered, on HIGH for 3 to 5 minutes or till heated, stirring after every 2 minutes. If desired, serve with decorative toothpicks. Serves 6.

Bacon-Wrapped Snacks

Whatever you please, you choose which tasty snack to wrap.

2 slices bacon, halved crosswise
1 chicken liver, quartered; 4 fresh *or* frozen shelled medium shrimp, thawed and deveined; 4 frozen fried potato nuggets, thawed; 4 whole water chestnuts; *or* 2 thin breadsticks, halved

● Place bacon on a plate between paper towels. Cook on HIGH for 1½ to 2 minutes or till bacon begins to brown but is still pliable, rotating plate a half-turn after 1 minute.

● Wrap *1* piece of bacon around *each* piece of chicken liver or desired filling. Secure with a wooden toothpick. Arrange the bacon-wrapped fillings on the plate between paper towels. Then cook on HIGH for 1 to 2 minutes or till fillings and bacon are done, rotating plate a half-turn after 1 minute. If desired, change wooden toothpicks to decorative toothpicks before serving. Makes 2 servings.

Parmesan Snack Crackers

Slip a favorite movie into your VCR and grab a handful of these cheesy snacks for nibbling.

½ cup margarine *or* butter
¼ cup grated Parmesan cheese
½ teaspoon celery salt
½ teaspoon paprika
¼ teaspoon garlic powder *or* onion powder
½ of a 16-ounce package (5 cups) oyster crackers

● In a 2-quart casserole or bowl place margarine or butter. Cook, uncovered, on HIGH for 1½ to 3 minutes or till melted.

● Stir in Parmesan cheese, celery salt, paprika, and garlic powder or onion powder. Add crackers, then toss till coated.

● Cook, uncovered, on HIGH for 3 minutes, stirring after every minute. Then spread on paper towels to cool. Transfer to a tightly covered container. Label and store at room temperature for up to 1 week. Makes 10 (½-cup) servings.

Bacon-Wrapped Snacks

Sugar- and Nut-
Glazed Brie
(see recipe, page 11)

Maple-Glazed
Sausage Links

Parmesan Snack Crackers

English Muffin Fix-Ups

Mini, open-face sandwiches that'll tide you over until dinner.

1 toasted English muffin half
   or plain bagel half
Desired topping
   (see below)

● Prepare English muffin or bagel half with desired topping as directed below. Place on a small plate or paper towel. Then cook, uncovered, on HIGH as directed. Makes 1 serving.

Ham 'n' Cheese Topping: Stir together 1 tablespoon soft-style *cream cheese* (plain, with chives and onion, *or* with pineapple) and 1 tablespoon very finely chopped, fully cooked *ham*. Spread on muffin or bagel. Cook for 15 to 25 seconds or till warm.

Tangy Havarti Topping: Spread muffin or bagel with *Dijon-style mustard*. Sprinkle with 1 teaspoon chopped *sun-dried tomatoes* (if desired), then sprinkle with 2 tablespoons shredded *Havarti or Monterey Jack cheese*. Cook for 15 to 25 seconds or just till cheese is melted.

Pizza Topping: Spread English muffin or bagel half with 1 tablespoon canned *pizza sauce*. Sprinkle with 1 tablespoon very finely chopped *pepperoni* (if desired), then sprinkle with 2 tablespoons shredded *mozzarella or provolone cheese*. Cook for 15 to 25 seconds or till cheese is just melted.

Bacon-Cheese Potato Slices

Use either potato slices for Irish-style nachos or tortilla chips for Mexican-style nachos.

1 medium baking potato
   (about 8 ounces)
1 small green onion, thinly
   sliced
½ cup shredded sharp
   cheddar cheese,
   Monterey Jack,
   or Monterey Jack with
   jalapeño peppers
2 tablespoons cooked bacon
   pieces *or* 2 slices bacon,
   crisp-cooked, drained,
   and crumbled (see chart,
   page 70)
1 tablespoon sliced pitted
   ripe olives

● Scrub potato, then trim ends. Cut the potato crosswise into ⅜-inch-thick slices. Arrange slices in a single layer on a medium-size dinner plate. Sprinkle with onion. Then cover with vented plastic wrap. Cook on HIGH for 7 to 9 minutes or till potato is tender, rotating plate a half-turn after 4 minutes.

● Sprinkle with cheese, bacon, and olives. Cook, uncovered, on HIGH for 30 seconds to 1½ minutes or just till cheese begins to melt. Makes 2 servings.

Bacon-Cheese Nachos: Omit potato and onion. Spread 2 cups (2½ ounces) *tortilla chips* on the plate. Sprinkle with ¾ *cup* cheese. Then sprinkle with bacon and olives as directed above, and 2 tablespoons canned chopped *green chili peppers or jalapeño chili peppers.*

● Cook, uncovered, on HIGH for 1 to 1½ minutes or just till cheese begins to melt. If desired, drizzle with ¼ cup *salsa* and serve with thawed frozen *avocado dip or* dairy *sour cream.*

Quesadilla

1 6- *or* 7-inch flour tortilla
¼ cup shredded Monterey Jack cheese with jalapeño peppers, *or* ¼ cup cheddar cheese *plus* 1 tablespoon canned chopped green chili peppers
  Frozen avocado dip, thawed, *or* dairy sour cream (optional)
  Slice pitted ripe olives (optional)

● Place tortilla on a small plate or paper plate. Sprinkle *half* of the tortilla with pepper cheese or with cheese and chili peppers. Fold plain tortilla half over top of cheese, pressing down gently to close. Cover with damp paper towel. Cook on HIGH for 30 seconds to 1½ minutes or just till cheese is melted.

● To serve, cut into 2 or 3 triangles. If desired, top with avocado dip or sour cream, and olives. Makes 1 or 2 servings.

Chicken Quesadilla: Prepare Quesadilla as directed above, *except* sprinkle 1 slice chopped *chicken or turkey luncheon meat* on top of the cheese.

Bean Quesadilla: Prepare Quesadilla as directed above, *except* spread tortilla with 2 tablespoons canned *bean dip* before sprinkling with the cheese.

Veggie-Topped Crackers

Our editors liked cauliflower, broccoli, and carrot as toppings in this cheesy snack.

2 tablespoons soft-style cream cheese with chives and onion
1 tablespoon shredded Monterey Jack *or* mozzarella cheese
3 tablespoons very finely chopped *or* coarsely shredded fresh vegetables
2 3- to 3½-inch-round lahvosh crackers

● In a small mixing bowl stir together cream cheese and shredded cheese. Then stir in chopped or shredded vegetables.

● Spread cheese mixture evenly on crackers. Place crackers on a small plate or paper plate. Cook, uncovered, on HIGH for 30 to 45 seconds or till cheese is softened and heated. Serves 1.

Chili con Queso Dip

8 ounces American cheese, cubed
½ cup hot salsa
¼ cup beer *or* milk
2 tablespoons chopped ripe olives
  Tortilla chips *or* assorted cut-up fresh vegetables

● In a 1-quart casserole or bowl combine cheese, salsa, and beer or milk. Cook, covered, on HIGH for 5 to 8 minutes or till cheese is melted and mixture is heated, stirring after every 2 minutes. Stir in olives.

● If desired, garnish dip with chopped tomato or sliced green onion. Serve dip with tortilla chips or vegetables as dippers. Makes 6 (¼-cup) servings.

S'More

One thousand one, one thousand two.... If your oven timer doesn't have second increments, then check your watch, or just count.

2 graham cracker squares
　or two 2- to 3-inch-round
　chocolate chip cookies
¼ of a 1½- to 2-ounce bar
　milk chocolate
1 large marshmallow, halved

● Place *1* cracker square or cookie on a small plate or paper plate. Top with chocolate and marshmallow, then top with remaining cracker square or cookie.

● Cook, uncovered, on HIGH for 10 to 20 seconds or till marshmallow puffs and softens slightly. Let cool a few seconds before eating. Makes 1 serving.

Peanut Butter S'More: Prepare S'More as directed above, *except* spread the bottom cracker square or cookie with some *peanut butter.*

Apricot-Bran Muffins

Muffins for now and muffins for later: This batter will keep for up to 1 week in a tightly covered container in the refrigerator.

1 beaten egg
⅓ cup buttermilk *or* sour
　milk
2 tablespoons brown sugar
1 tablespoon cooking oil
¼ cup whole bran cereal
½ cup all-purpose flour
½ teaspoon baking powder
¼ teaspoon baking soda
¼ teaspoon ground cinnamon
¼ teaspoon ground nutmeg
　Dash salt
¼ cup snipped dried apricots
1 tablespoon toasted
　wheat germ
1 tablespoon finely chopped
　nuts
1 tablespoon brown sugar

● In a medium mixing bowl combine egg, buttermilk or sour milk, 2 tablespoons brown sugar, and oil. Stir in cereal, then let stand for 5 minutes. In another bowl combine flour, baking powder, soda, cinnamon, nutmeg, and salt. Then add to bran mixture. Stir just till moistened. Fold in apricots.

● For wheat germ topping, in a small mixing bowl stir together wheat germ, nuts, and 1 tablespoon brown sugar.

● Line 6-ounce custard cups or a microwave-safe muffin pan with paper bake cups. For *each* of the muffins, spoon about *2 tablespoons* batter into a prepared cup. Then sprinkle with about *1 teaspoon* wheat germ topping.

● If using custard cups, arrange them in a circle. Cook *6* muffins, uncovered, on HIGH for 2 to 3 minutes or till muffins have a crumb texture when surfaces are scratched with a toothpick, rearranging cups or rotating pan a half-turn after every minute. If using custard cups, remove each cup from oven when done. (For *4* muffins, cook 1 to 1½ minutes; for *2* muffins, cook 45 seconds to 1 minute; for *1* muffin, cook 30 to 40 seconds.) Remove muffins from cups or pan. Let stand on a wire rack for 5 minutes. Serve warm. Makes about 6.

Easy Main Dishes

Planning dinner for one or two? A family affair? No matter which, you'll find a smorgasbord of hassle-free mealtime ideas in this chapter. Choose from hearty and homey favorites or light and elegant entrées. All are simple to prepare in your low-wattage microwave oven.

Easy Main-Dish Tips

The Cover-Up

Solve the mystery of when to cover foods during microwave cooking by following this rule of thumb: Cover any food in the microwave that you would cover during conventional cooking. Use the following guidelines in choosing from the many types of covers:

● **Paper towels** work well for cooking bacon or reheating breads, rolls, and items with crisp crusts.

The paper absorbs moisture, allows steam to escape, and prevents fats from spattering (see photo, page 70). Be sure to choose undyed towels. The dyes in colored paper towels may leak onto the food.

● **Waxed paper** holds in more heat than paper towels but won't cause the food to steam. Use it for foods that spatter and meats that don't need tenderizing, such as poultry.

● **Lids** or **vented plastic wrap** create a tighter seal than paper towels or waxed paper, holding the steam inside so that it can evenly surround the food.

Leave an air space between the food and wrap (see photo, page 50).

Always be sure to use *microwave-safe* plastic wrap. It's designed to withstand higher temperatures than regular plastic wrap.

Speed Up Your Cookout

Mmm—you long for barbecued food, but don't want to take hours to grill. Then let your microwave oven help cut your grilling time. Place the food in a round baking dish. Cook on HIGH, then grill, uncovered, directly over *medium* coals, as directed below.

Chicken: In the dish arrange *1 to 1½ pounds meaty chicken pieces*, skin sides down, with meaty portions toward edges of dish. Cover with waxed paper. Cook for 6 minutes, rotating pieces after 3 minutes so outside edges face center and then rotating dish a quarter-turn. Grill, skin side down, for 8 to 10 minutes or till no longer pink, turning pieces over after 5 minutes.

Pork chops: Place *2 pork loin rib chops*, cut 1½ inches thick (about 1¼ pounds) in the dish. Cover with vented plastic wrap. Cook for 9 minutes, turning over after 5 minutes so outside edges face center and then rotating dish a quarter-turn. Grill for 7 to 10 minutes or till no longer pink, turning chops over after 5 minutes.

Bratwursts, or Polish or Italian sausage links: Place *1 pound fresh sausage* in the dish. Prick skins several times with a fork. Cover with vented plastic wrap. Cook for 7 minutes, rearranging after 4 minutes by moving outside links to center and then rotating dish a quarter-turn. Grill for 6 to 8 minutes or till done, turning sausage over after 4 minutes.

Individual Meat Loaves

A three-ingredient meat loaf in minutes.

1 single-serving-size envelope
    instant onion *or*
    vegetable-beef soup mix
1 tablespoon milk
8 ounces lean ground beef
    or ground raw turkey
1 tablespoon catsup, bottled
    barbecue sauce, steak
    sauce, *or* chili sauce
    (optional)

● In a bowl stir together soup mix and milk. Add ground beef or turkey and mix well. Shape mixture into *two* 3½x2-inch loaves. Place on a medium-size dinner plate. Cover with waxed paper.

● Cook on HIGH for 3 minutes. Rotate meat loaves on plate so outside edges face center of plate. Then cook, covered, on HIGH for 1½ to 4½ minutes more or till no longer pink and meat is well-done (170°). Let stand for 2 minutes.

● To serve, transfer meat loaves to a platter. If desired, brush with catsup or desired sauce. Makes 2 servings.

Burgers: Prepare Individual Meat Loaves as directed above, *except* form meat mixture into two ¾-inch-thick patties. Place patties on a medium-size dinner plate. Cover with waxed paper. Cook on HIGH for 4½ to 7½ minutes or till done, turning over after 3 minutes so outside edges face center, then rotating plate a half-turn. Meanwhile, split and toast 2 *hamburger buns*.
● To serve, brush patties with catsup or desired sauce. Place patties on bun bottoms, then top with *onion slices, tomato slices, lettuce,* and bun tops.

Beefed-Up Vegetable Soup

Some like it hot and some do not: For a peppy soup, choose the hot-style juice cocktail.

8 ounces lean ground beef
    or ground raw turkey
½ cup chopped seeded
    cucumber
1½ cups vegetable juice
    cocktail *or* hot-style
    vegetable juice
    cocktail
1 8-ounce can stewed
    tomatoes
1 teaspoon Worcestershire
    sauce
½ teaspoon instant beef
    bouillon granules
¼ teaspoon dried basil,
    crushed (optional)

● In a 1½-quart casserole combine loose ground beef or turkey and cucumber. Cook, covered, on HIGH for 4 to 6 minutes or till no longer pink, stirring after every 2 minutes. Drain off juices.

● Stir in the vegetable juice cocktail, *undrained* tomatoes, Worcestershire sauce, bouillon granules, and basil, if desired. Cook, covered, on HIGH for 7 to 10 minutes more or till heated. Makes 3 servings.

Easy Chili con Carne

Spoon sour cream and cheddar cheese on this fast-fixing chili to make it extra good.

8 ounces lean ground beef
   or ground raw turkey
1 14½-ounce can stewed
   tomatoes
1 8-ounce can red kidney
   beans, drained
⅓ cup salsa
1 tablespoon chili powder

● Place loose ground beef or turkey in a 1-quart casserole. Cook, covered, on HIGH for 3½ to 5 minutes or till no longer pink, stirring after every 2 minutes. Drain off juices.

● Stir in *undrained* tomatoes, beans, salsa, and chili powder. Cook, covered, on HIGH for 6 to 8 minutes more or till boiling, stirring after every 3 minutes. Makes 2 or 3 servings.

Beef-Asparagus Rolls with Mustard Sauce

Elegant enough for company, yet homey enough for the family.

1 10-ounce package frozen
   asparagus spears
1 pound beef top round
   steak, cut ½ inch thick,
   or four 6-ounce beef
   cubed steaks
¼ teaspoon garlic salt
¼ teaspoon dried rosemary
   or basil, crushed
   Soy sauce (optional)
½ of an 8-ounce container
   (about ½ cup) soft-style
   cream cheese
2 tablespoons milk
2 tablespoons Dijon-style
   mustard
   Hot cooked rice
   Snipped chives

● Place unwrapped asparagus on a plate. Cover with vented plastic wrap. Cook on HIGH for 2½ to 4½ minutes or just till thawed, breaking spears apart after 2 minutes. Drain well.

● If using round steak, cut it into *4* pieces. Working from the center to edges, pound *each* piece with the coarse-tooth side of a meat mallet to form rectangles ¼ inch thick.

● For rolls, sprinkle one side of *each* piece of round steak or cubed steak with garlic salt and rosemary or basil. Place asparagus on one edge of the seasoned side of *each* steak portion. Roll meat around vegetable. Secure with wooden toothpicks. Place rolls, seam side down, in a 9-inch pie plate. If desired, brush with soy sauce. Cover with waxed paper. Cook on HIGH for 8 to 12 minutes or just till no pink remains, rearranging after 5 minutes by moving outside rolls to center and then rotating dish a quarter-turn. Keep covered.

● For sauce, in a small bowl stir together cream cheese, milk, and mustard. Cook, uncovered, on HIGH for 1 to 2 minutes or just till heated, stirring after 1 minute. Stir till smooth.

● To serve, remove toothpicks from rolls. Place on rice, then spoon sauce over rolls. Sprinkle with chives. Makes 4 servings.

For a very small cavity oven: Use *half* of the amount of *each* ingredient. Prepare as above, *except* cook asparagus, covered, on HIGH for 1½ to 3 minutes or just till thawed. Place meat-vegetable rolls in a 1½-quart casserole. Cook, covered, on HIGH for 5 to 9 minutes or just till done, rearranging rolls after 3 minutes. Cook sauce, uncovered, on HIGH for 1 to 1½ minutes or just till heated. Serve as above. Makes 2 servings.

Beef-Asparagus Rolls
with Mustard Sauce

Swiss Cubed Steaks

Good old-fashioned flavor from the microwave.

2 tablespoons all-purpose
flour
2 5- to 6-ounce beef cubed
steaks
½ of a single-serving-size
envelope (1½ teaspoons)
instant onion soup mix
Pepper
½ cup tomato sauce
2 tablespoons finely chopped
green pepper

● Place flour on waxed paper. Dip cubed steaks in flour to coat. Place steaks in a single layer in 9-inch pie plate. Sprinkle steaks with dry soup mix. Then sprinkle with pepper.

● In a 1-cup measure stir together tomato sauce and green pepper. Pour sauce mixture over steaks. Cover with vented plastic wrap. Cook on HIGH for 3 minutes. Rotate steaks in pie plate so outside edges face center of pie plate and then rotate pie plate a quarter-turn. Cook, covered, on HIGH for 3 to 5 minutes more or till steaks are no longer pink. Makes 2 servings.

For a very small cavity oven: Use *1 tablespoon* all-purpose flour, *one* 5- to 6-ounce beef cubed steak, *1 teaspoon* instant onion soup mix, *dash* pepper, *¼ cup* tomato sauce, and *1 tablespoon* finely chopped green pepper.
● Prepare as directed above, *except* place steak in a 1-quart casserole. Cook, covered, on HIGH for 4 to 5 minutes or till steak is done, rotating casserole a quarter-turn after 2 minutes. Makes 1 serving.

Beef Stroganoff

For a delightful dill flavor, stir in ¼ teaspoon dried dillweed.

8 ounces boneless beef sirloin
steak *or* beef top loin
steak
1 7½-ounce can semi-
condensed cream of
mushroom soup
1 4-ounce can sliced
mushrooms, drained
1 tablespoon dry white wine
(optional)
1 teaspoon dried minced
onion
⅓ cup dairy sour cream
or plain yogurt
Hot cooked noodles

● Place meat in the freezer about 45 minutes or till *partially* frozen. Thinly slice meat across the grain into bite-size strips.

● Place meat in a 1½-quart casserole. Cook, covered, on HIGH for 3 to 5 minutes or till no longer pink, stirring after every 2 minutes. Drain off juices.

● Stir semicondensed soup, mushrooms, wine (if desired), and dried onion into meat in casserole. Then cook, covered, on HIGH for 4 to 5 minutes or till heated, stirring after 3 minutes.

● Stir some of the hot meat mixture into the sour cream or yogurt. Then return sour cream mixture to the casserole. Cook, covered, on HIGH for 1 to 2 minutes more or till heated. Serve over hot cooked noodles. Makes 2 or 3 servings.

Beef Stir-Fry

8 ounces boneless beef sirloin
   steak *or* beef top loin
   steak
2 tablespoons teriyaki sauce
2 tablespoons water
1 tablespoon cornstarch
¾ cup sliced fresh
   mushrooms
6 green onions, bias-sliced
   into 1-inch pieces
1 tablespoon water
1 teaspoon grated gingerroot
   or ¼ teaspoon ground
   ginger
1 clove garlic, minced, *or*
   ⅛ teaspoon garlic powder
6 cherry tomatoes, halved
   Hot cooked rice *or*
   couscous*

● Place meat in the freezer about 45 minutes or till *partially* frozen. Thinly slice meat across the grain into bite-size strips. In a custard cup stir together teriyaki sauce, 2 tablespoons water, and cornstarch. Set teriyaki sauce mixture aside.

● In a 1½-quart casserole combine mushrooms, onions, and 1 tablespoon water. Cook, covered, on HIGH for 3 to 5 minutes till vegetables are nearly tender, stirring after 2 minutes. Drain, then set vegetables aside.

● In the casserole combine meat, ginger, and garlic. Cook, covered, on HIGH for 3 to 5 minutes or till meat is no longer pink, stirring after every 2 minutes. *Do not drain off juices.* Stir in teriyaki mixture. Cook, uncovered, on HIGH for 1 minute. Stir. Then cook, uncovered, on HIGH for 1 to 3 minutes more or till thickened and bubbly, stirring after every 30 seconds.

● Stir in vegetables and cherry tomatoes. Cook, uncovered, on HIGH for 30 to 60 seconds or till heated. Serve over hot cooked rice or couscous. Makes 2 or 3 servings.

*To cook couscous in the microwave oven: In 2-cup measure combine ¾ cup *hot water* and ¼ teaspoon *salt.* Then cook, uncovered, on HIGH for 3 to 4 minutes or till boiling. Stir in ½ cup quick-cooking *couscous.* Let stand, covered, for 5 minutes or while cooking meat-vegetable mixture.

Reuben Sandwiches

Put away the griddle and open the microwave door. Here's a no-mess method for this classic grilled sandwich.

6 ounces thinly sliced corned
   beef
¼ cup sauerkraut, rinsed and
   drained
2 slices Swiss cheese
4 slices rye *or* pumpernickel
   bread, toasted
   Thousand Island salad
   dressing, horseradish
   mustard, *or* coarse-grain
   brown mustard

● On a medium-size dinner plate mound corned beef in *2* piles. Top each pile of meat with the sauerkraut. Cook, uncovered, on HIGH for 3 to 4 minutes or till heated.

● Top each pile with a cheese slice. Then cook, uncovered, on HIGH for 1 to 2 minutes more or till cheese is melted.

● Meanwhile, place toasted bread on individual plates. Spread one side of bread slices with salad dressing or mustard.

● To serve, use a wide spatula to transfer each mound of meat to the dressing side of *2* bread slices. Top with remaining bread slices, dressing-side down. Makes 2 servings.

Ham with Orange-Raisin Sauce

2 3-ounce slices fully cooked boneless ham slices, cut about ½ inch thick
2 teaspoons cornstarch
1 teaspoon brown sugar
¼ teaspoon instant chicken bouillon granules
½ cup orange juice
2 tablespoons raisins
½ teaspoon prepared horseradish

● Place ham in a 7-inch pie plate or 1½-quart casserole. Cover with waxed paper. Cook on HIGH for 3 to 4 minutes or till heated, turning slices over after 2 mintues so outside edges face center and then rotating dish a quarter-turn. Keep covered.

● For sauce, in a 2-cup measure stir together cornstarch, brown sugar, and bouillon granules. Stir in juice, raisins, and horseradish. Cook, uncovered, on HIGH for 1 minute. Stir. Then cook, uncovered, on HIGH for 1 to 2 minutes more or till thickened and bubbly, stirring after every 30 seconds. Transfer ham to a serving platter. Pour sauce over ham. Serves 2.

Maple- and Nut-Glazed Ham

Always toast at least ½ cup of nuts at a time, because smaller amounts will burn. (See Micro-Cooking Tips, page 78.) Save the extra nuts for another use.

2 tablespoons maple-flavored syrup
1 tablespoon finely chopped walnuts (toasted, if desired)
1 teaspoon Dijon-style mustard
1 8-ounce fully cooked boneless ham slice, cut about ½ inch thick

● For glaze mixture, in a custard cup stir together maple syrup, walnuts, and mustard. Set glaze mixture aside.

● Cut ham in half. Place in a 1½-quart casserole. Cover with waxed paper. Cook on HIGH for 3 minutes. Turn ham over so outside edges face center. Brush with glaze. Cook, uncovered, for 2 to 3 minutes or till heated. Transfer to a platter. Serves 2.

Maple- and Nut-Glazed Chops: Prepare Maple- and Nut-Glazed Chops as directed above, *except* substitute two 5- to 6-ounce *smoked pork loin chops*, cut ½ inch thick, for the ham.

German-Style Bologna Casserole

A hearty dinner for four in just 12 minutes.

1 1-pound ring bologna, halved, *or* 1 pound fully cooked bratwursts *or* Polish sausages
1 15½-ounce can German-style potato salad
1 small apple, chopped (about ½ cup)
2 tablespoons snipped parsley

● Cut the bologna pieces lengthwise in half, then slice into ½-inch pieces. *Or,* slice the bratwursts or Polish sausages into ½-inch pieces.

● In a 1½-quart casserole gently toss together meat, potato salad, and apple. Cook, covered, on HIGH for 8 to 10 minutes or till heated, gently stirring after every 3 minutes. Sprinkle with parsley. Makes 4 servings.

Sweet 'n' Sour Pork

1 8-ounce can pineapple
    tidbits (juice pack)
8 ounces boneless pork
1½ cups loose-pack frozen
    broccoli, carrots, water
    chestnuts, and red
    peppers
3 tablespoons cider vinegar
    or red wine vinegar
2 tablespoons soy sauce
1 tablespoon cornstarch
1 tablespoon sugar
1 teaspoon instant chicken
    bouillon granules
    Hot cooked rice
    Sliced almonds, toasted
    (see Micro-Cooking Tips,
    page 78) (optional)

● Drain the pineapple, reserving juice. (You should have about ⅓ *cup* of juice.) Set aside.

● Place meat in the freezer about 45 minutes or till *partially* frozen. Thinly slice meat across the grain into bite-size strips. Place in a 1½-quart casserole. Cook, covered, on HIGH for 3 to 5 minutes or till no longer pink. Drain and set meat aside.

● Place frozen vegetables in the casserole. Cook, covered, on HIGH for 4 to 6 minutes or till tender. Drain, then add meat and pineapple to the casserole. Cover and set aside.

● For sauce mixture, in a 2-cup measure combine the reserved juice, vinegar, soy sauce, cornstarch, sugar, and bouillon granules. Cook, uncovered, on HIGH for 2 to 4 minutes or till thickened and bubbly, stirring after every minute.

● Stir sauce mixture into vegetable mixture in casserole. Cook, uncovered, on HIGH for 2 to 4 minutes or till heated. Serve over hot cooked rice. If desired, garnish with almonds. Serves 3.

Spicy Meatball Sandwiches

Meatballs in a bun—these saucy sandwiches are popular with kids and adults alike.

2 6-inch-long French-style
    rolls
2 tablespoons milk
8 ounces bulk Italian sausage
¼ cup chopped green pepper
½ cup spaghetti sauce with
    mushrooms
2 tablespoons finely
    shredded *or* grated
    Parmesan cheese

● For bread shells, cut a thin lengthwise slice from the top of *each* roll. Hollow out the bottom portion of each roll, leaving a ½-inch-thick shell. Tear bread from insides of shells and top slices into pea-size pieces. Measure ¼ *cup* of the torn bread. (Reserve remaining bread for another use.)

● In a medium mixing bowl stir together the ¼ cup torn bread and milk. Add sausage and mix well. Then shape meat mixture into *8* meatballs. Place meatballs in a single layer in a 1½-quart casserole. Then add green pepper to casserole. Cook, covered, on HIGH for 4 to 6 minutes or till meatballs are evenly browned and juices are clear when the meatballs are poked with a fork, rotating the casserole a half-turn after every 2 minutes. Drain off the juices.

● Add spaghetti sauce to meatballs in casserole. Gently stir till meatballs are coated. Then cook, covered, on HIGH for 1½ to 2 minutes or till heated, stirring after 1 minute.

● To serve, spoon *4* meatballs and some sauce into *each* roll. Sprinkle with cheese. Makes 2 servings.

Fruit-Stuffed Cornish Hen

Fruit-Stuffed Cornish Hen

A festive entrée for two.

1 1- to 1½-pound frozen
   Cornish game hen
1 cup chilled cooked rice
⅓ cup prepared mincemeat
¼ cup finely chopped apple
   or celery
2 tablespoons chopped
   walnuts
   Dash salt
2 tablespoons orange
   marmalade *or* apple jelly
1 teaspoon soy sauce
   Dash ground ginger
   Apple slices (optional)
   Fresh sage leaves (optional)

● Thaw the Cornish hen (see chart, page 66). Meanwhile, for stuffing, in a small bowl combine the rice, mincemeat, chopped apple or celery, walnuts, and salt.

● Rinse hen, then pat dry. Spoon *half* of the stuffing (about ¾ cup) loosely into the body cavity. Put remaining stuffing in an individual casserole; set aside. Tie legs of hen to tail; twist wing tips under back. Place hen, breast side down, on a microwave-safe rack in an 8x8x2-inch baking dish. *Or,* place hen, breast side down, in a 1½-quart casserole without a rack.

● In a custard cup stir together marmalade or jelly, soy sauce, and ginger. If necessary, cook on HIGH for 30 to 60 seconds or till melted. Then brush some of the mixture onto the hen.

● Loosely cover hen with waxed paper. Cook on HIGH for 13 to 15 minutes or till done, turning bird breast side up and brushing with more of the marmalade or jelly mixture after 6 minutes. (Hen is done when drumsticks move easily in their sockets.) Let stand, loosely covered, for 5 minutes.

● Meanwhile, cook stuffing in casserole, covered, on HIGH for 2 to 3 minutes or till heated.

● To serve, transfer stuffing from casserole to a platter. Place hen on top. Brush hen with remaining marmalade or jelly mixture. If desired, garnish with apple slices and sage. Serves 2.

Parmesan Drumsticks

2 tablespoons fine dry
   seasoned bread crumbs
1 tablespoon grated
   Parmesan cheese
⅛ teaspoon garlic powder
⅛ teaspoon paprika
4 chicken drumsticks
   (¾ to 1 pound)
1 to 2 tablespoons milk

● On waxed paper combine bread crumbs, Parmesan cheese, garlic powder, and paprika.

● Rinse drumsticks, then pat dry. Brush drumsticks with milk. Then dip one side of drumsticks into crumb mixture, leaving the other side uncoated. (If you coat both sides with crumbs, the coating on the bottom will get soggy.)

● On a medium-size dinner plate arrange drumsticks, coated side up, in a spoke fashion with meaty ends toward edges of the plate. Sprinkle with any remaining crumb mixture. Cover with a paper towel. Cook on HIGH for 7 to 9 minutes or till no longer pink, rotating plate a half-turn after 5 minutes. Serves 2.

Turkey Cordon Bleu

2 tablespoons finely crushed cornflakes *or* fine dry bread crumbs
½ teaspoon dried parsley flakes
1 8- to 10-ounce turkey tenderloin
1 teaspoon Dijon-style mustard
1 thin slice fully cooked ham
1 slice Swiss cheese (1 to 1½ ounces)

● On waxed paper combine crushed cornflakes or bread crumbs and parsley, then set aside.

● To assemble, cut a lengthwise slit in the side of the turkey tenderloin to within ½ inch of opposite side, forming a pocket. Spread mustard in pocket. Roll slice of ham and cheese together, then place it in the pocket of the tenderloin. Secure tenderloin with wooden toothpicks.

● If necessary, dampen top side of turkey tenderloin lightly with *water* so crumbs will stick. Then dip the top side of turkey tenderloin in crumb mixture, leaving bottom side uncoated. (If you coat both sides with crumbs, the coating on the bottom will get soggy.)

● Place stuffed tenderloin, coated side up, on a medium-size dinner plate. Sprinkle with any remaining crumbs. Cover with a paper towel. Cook on HIGH for 8 to 11 minutes or till no longer pink, rotating plate a half-turn after 5 minutes. Remove toothpicks before serving. Makes 2 servings.

Chicken Fajitas

8 ounces boned skinless chicken breast halves *or* turkey tenderloin steaks
2 tablespoons sliced green onion
Chunky salsa
4 6-inch flour tortillas
¼ cup dairy sour cream
¼ cup frozen avocado dip, thawed

● For filling, cut chicken or turkey into thin bite-size strips. Place poultry and green onion in a 1-quart casserole. Cook, covered, on HIGH for 3 to 5 minutes or *just* till poultry is no longer pink, stirring after every 2 minutes. Drain off juices, then stir *2 tablespoons* salsa into poultry mixture. Cook, covered, on HIGH for 1 to 2 minutes more or till heated. Keep covered.

● Heat tortillas (see chart, page 74).

● To serve, using a slotted spoon, spoon poultry mixture across the center of each tortilla. Then top with sour cream and avocado dip. Roll tortilla around meat and toppings. Serve with additional salsa. Makes 2 servings.

Chicken Tacos: Omit tortillas. Prepare the poultry filling as directed above.
● To serve, place ½ cup finely shredded *lettuce* in 6 *taco shells.* Using a slotted spoon, spoon poultry mixture on top of lettuce. Then top with ½ of a small *tomato,* chopped; sour cream (if desired); avocado dip (if desired); and ¼ cup finely shredded *cheddar cheese* (1 ounce). If desired, serve with additional salsa. Makes 2 or 3 servings.

Tuna 'n' Apple Tater Melts

A complete meal in one: stuffed potatoes chock-full of apple, cheese, and tuna.

2 medium baking potatoes (6 to 8 ounces each)
1 6½-ounce can tuna (water pack), drained and flaked
¼ cup chopped apple
¼ cup mayonnaise *or* salad dressing
2 tablespoons thinly sliced green onion
¼ cup finely shredded cheddar cheese (1 ounce)

● Scrub potatoes. Prick several times with a fork. Place potatoes on a plate. Cook, uncovered, on HIGH for 11 to 13 minutes or till tender, rotating plate a quarter-turn after 6 minutes. Let potatoes stand while cooking filling.

● Meanwhile, for filling, in a small bowl gently stir together tuna, apple, mayonnaise or salad dressing, green onion, and *half* of the cheese. Cook, uncovered, on HIGH for 2 to 3 minutes or till heated, gently stirring after 1 minute.

● To serve, transfer the potatoes to individual plates. Cut a lengthwise slit in the top of each potato. Slightly open slits and fluff pulp with a fork. Then spoon the hot tuna mixture into the potatoes. Sprinkle with remaining cheese. Makes 2 servings.

Tuna 'n' Apple Muffin Melts: Omit potatoes. Prepare filling as directed above.
● To serve, place 2 toasted and split *English muffins* on individual plates. Spoon hot tuna mixture on top of muffin halves. Sprinkle with remaining cheese.

Jiffy Seafood Casserole

There's no need to cook the noodles before adding them to this easy casserole.

1 10¾- *or* 13-ounce can ready-to-eat New England-style clam chowder
1 cup finely shredded cheddar cheese (4 ounces)
½ cup frozen mixed vegetables
2 tablespoons diced pimiento (optional)
⅛ teaspoon pepper
1 7½-ounce can salmon, drained and skin and bones removed, *or* one 6½-ounce can tuna (water pack), drained
2 ounces (1 cup) egg noodles
¼ cup dairy sour cream
Snipped parsley (optional)
Sliced tomato (optional)

● In a 1½-quart casserole stir together soup, cheese, frozen vegetables, pimiento (if desired), and pepper.

● Break salmon or tuna into large chunks, then add it to soup mixture in casserole. Add *uncooked* noodles. Gently toss till mixed (mixture will appear dry).

● Cook, covered, on HIGH for 14 to 16 minutes or till noodles are tender, gently stirring after every 5 minutes. Gently stir in sour cream. If desired, sprinkle with snipped parsley and garnish with tomato. Makes 3 servings.

Butter-Almond Fish

A simple fish fix-up with a citrus flavor.

1 pound fresh *or* frozen
skinless fish fillets
(about ½ inch thick),
or fresh *or* frozen fish
steaks, cut ¾ to 1 inch
thick

2 tablespoons butter
or margarine

2 teaspoons lemon *or* lime
juice

2 tablespoons sliced
almonds, toasted (see
Micro-Cooking Tips,
page 78)

● Thaw fish, if frozen (see chart, page 66). For fillets: place fish in a single layer in an 8x8x2-inch baking dish, turning under any thin edges so total thickness is about ½ inch. Cover with vented plastic wrap. Cook on HIGH for 4 to 7 minutes or till fish flakes easily when tested with a fork, rotating dish a half-turn after 3 minutes. (For fish steaks: cook, covered, on HIGH for 4 to 7 minutes or till done, turning fish over after 2 minutes so outside edges face center and then rotate dish a half-turn.) Using a slotted spatula, transfer the fish to a serving platter. Then cover to keep warm.

● Place the butter or margarine in a custard cup. Cook, uncovered, on HIGH for 45 seconds to 2 minutes or till melted. Stir in juice. To serve, drizzle butter mixture over fish, then sprinkle with almonds. Makes 4 servings.

For a very small cavity oven: Use *8 ounces* fresh or frozen fish, *1 tablespoon* butter or margarine, *1 teaspoon* lemon or lime juice, and *1 tablespoon* toasted sliced almonds.
● Prepare as above, *except* place fish in a 1½-quart casserole. For fillets: cook fish, covered, on HIGH for 2½ to 5 minutes or till done, rotating casserole a half-turn after 2 minutes. (For fish steaks: cook, covered, on HIGH for 2½ to 5 minutes or till done, turning fish over after 1½ minutes and then rotating casserole a half-turn.)
● Cook butter, uncovered, on HIGH for 20 to 40 seconds or till melted. Stir in juice, then serve as above. Makes 2 servings.

Vegetable-Topped Orange Roughy

4 ounces fresh *or* frozen
skinless orange roughy,
flounder, *or* pompano
fillet (about ½ inch
thick)

¾ cup loose-pack frozen
broccoli, baby carrots,
and water chestnuts

1 tablespoon margarine
or butter

¼ teaspoon finely shredded
lemon *or* orange peel

⅛ teaspoon ground ginger
Dash garlic powder

● Thaw the fish, if frozen (see chart, page 66). Place frozen vegetables in a colander. Run *hot water* over vegetables just till thawed. Drain well, then pat dry with paper towels.

● Place margarine or butter in an individual casserole or 7-inch pie plate. Cook, uncovered, on HIGH for 20 to 40 seconds or till melted. Stir in lemon or orange peel, ginger, and garlic powder. Add fish to dish, turning fish over once to coat with margarine mixture. Then turn under any thin edges of fish so total thickness is about ½ inch. Top with vegetables.

● Cover with vented plastic wrap. Cook on HIGH for 2 to 4 minutes or till fish flakes easily when tested with a fork, rotating dish a half-turn after 2 minutes. Makes 1 serving.

Creamy Shrimp Bisque
(see recipe, page 32)

Creamy Shrimp Bisque

Transform a can of soup into an extraordinary bisque. (Pictured on page 31 and on cover.)

1   8-ounce package frozen
      peeled and deveined
      shrimp
1½ cups loose-pack frozen
      broccoli, cauliflower, and
      carrots
2   tablespoons water
1   3-ounce package cream
      cheese, softened (see
      Micro-Cooking Tips,
      page 77)
1   10¾-ounce can condensed
      cream of shrimp *or*
      cream of potato soup
1   cup milk
2   tablespoons dry sherry
      (optional)

● In a 1½-quart casserole combine the frozen shrimp and vegetables. Sprinkle with water. Cook, covered, on HIGH for 8 to 10 minutes or till shrimp turn pink and vegetables are tender, stirring after every 3 minutes. Drain in a colander; set aside.

● In the casserole stir together softened cream cheese and condensed soup. Then stir in milk and sherry, if desired. Cook, uncovered, on HIGH for 5 to 8 minutes or till hot and bubbly, stirring after 3 minutes. Stir in shrimp and vegetables. Cook, uncovered, on HIGH for 2 to 3 minutes or till heated. Serves 3.

Dijon Scallops on Rice

Have a hard day at work? Pamper yourself with this creamy scallop dish along with a tossed salad and a glass of wine. Ahhh—what a way to end the day.

8   ounces fresh *or* frozen
      scallops
½   cup sliced fresh
      mushrooms
2   tablespoons water
⅔   cup milk
1   tablespoon all-purpose
      flour
2   teaspoons Dijon-style
      mustard
½   teaspoon instant chicken
      bouillon granules
      Dash white pepper
1   cup hot cooked wild rice
      Snipped chives

● Thaw scallops, if frozen (see chart, page 66). Cut any large scallops crosswise in half.

● In a 1-quart casserole combine scallops and mushrooms. Sprinkle with water. Cook, covered, on HIGH for 2 to 3 minutes or till scallops are opaque, stirring after every minute. Drain in a colander, then transfer to a bowl. Cover to keep warm.

● For sauce, in the casserole stir together milk, flour, mustard, bouillon granules, and pepper till no lumps remain. Cook, uncovered, on HIGH for 4 to 5 minutes or till thickened and bubbly, stirring after every minute.

● Stir scallops and mushrooms into the sauce in the casserole. Cook, uncovered, on HIGH for 30 seconds to 1 minute or till mixture is heated.

● To serve, on individual plates spoon scallop mixture over rice. Sprinkle with chives. Makes 2 servings.

Brunch Scramble

¼ cup sliced green onion
1 small carrot, shredded,
    or ¼ cup chopped green
    pepper
1 tablespoon margarine
    or butter
4 beaten eggs
¼ cup milk
⅛ teaspoon salt
    Dash pepper

● In a 1-quart casserole combine onion, carrot or green pepper, and margarine or butter. Cook, covered, on HIGH for 2 to 4 minutes or till tender, stirring after 1 minute.

● Stir in beaten eggs, milk, salt, and pepper. Cook, uncovered, on HIGH for 3 to 6 minutes or till eggs are *almost* set, pushing cooked portions to center after 1½ and 3 minutes, then pushing cooked portions to center after every 30 seconds. Let stand, covered, about 2 minutes or till eggs are set. Makes 2 servings.

Denver Sandwiches: Prepare Brunch Scramble as directed above, *except* use the green pepper option and stir ½ cup finely chopped fully cooked *ham* into egg mixture in casserole.
● To serve, spoon mixture onto 2 slices buttered *toast.* Then top with 2 more slices buttered *toast. Or,* spoon mixture into 2 large *pita bread round halves.*

Brunch Burritos: Omit margarine or butter. In the casserole combine 4 ounces bulk *pork sausage or turkey sausage*, green onion, and carrot or green pepper. Cook, covered, on HIGH for 3½ to 4½ minutes or till meat is no longer pink and vegetables are tender, stirring after 2 minutes. Drain.
● Stir in beaten eggs, milk, salt, pepper, and ¼ teaspoon bottled *hot pepper sauce*. Cook egg mixture as above.
● To serve, spoon egg mixture across centers of two 7-inch *flour tortillas* (within 1 inch of one side.) Sprinkle with ¼ cup finely shredded *Monterey Jack or cheddar cheese* (1 ounce). Roll tortilla around filling and cheese. If desired, serve with *salsa.*

Cheese Omelet for One

2 eggs
2 tablespoons milk
1 teaspoon cooked bacon
    pieces *or* dash salt
    Dash pepper
2 tablespoons finely
    shredded cheddar cheese
    (½ ounce)
1 teaspoon margarine
    or butter

● In a small mixing bowl use a fork to beat eggs, milk, bacon pieces or salt, and pepper together till yolks and whites are well mixed. Then stir in *half* of the cheese and set aside.

● Place margarine or butter in a 7-inch pie plate or 1½-quart casserole. Cook, uncovered, on HIGH for 30 to 40 seconds or till melted. Tilt dish to coat it evenly with margarine. Pour in egg mixture. Cook, uncovered, on HIGH for 2 to 3 minutes or till eggs are set but still shiny and creamy, lifting cooked edges and letting uncooked portions flow underneath every 30 seconds.

● To serve, fold omelet in half, then slide it from dish onto a dinner plate. Sprinkle with remaining cheese. Makes 1 serving.

Country Egg Pie

Reminiscent of a quiche, but without the crust.

½ cup frozen loose-pack hash
　　brown potatoes
4 ounces bulk pork sausage
　　or turkey sausage
1 large green onion, thinly
　　sliced
4 eggs
¼ cup milk
½ cup shredded sharp
　　cheddar cheese
　　(2 ounces)
　　Chopped tomato (optional)

● Place frozen hash browns in a colander. Run *hot water* over potatoes just till thawed. Drain well, then set aside.

● In a 7-inch pie plate or quiche dish crumble loose bulk sausage into small pieces. Add potatoes and onion. Cover with vented plastic wrap. Cook on HIGH for 3 to 5 minutes or till sausage is no longer pink, stirring after every minute. Drain off juices, then spread sausage-potato mixture evenly in dish.

● In a small mixing bowl use a rotary beater to beat eggs and milk together. Stir in *half* of the cheese. Pour egg mixture over sausage-potato mixture in dish. Cook, uncovered, on HIGH for 3 to 4 minutes or till eggs are *almost* set, pushing cooked portions to center of dish after every minute and rotating dish a half-turn after 2 minutes.

● If desired, top with tomato. Then sprinkle with remaining cheese. Cook, uncovered, on HIGH for 1 to 2 minutes or just till cheese begins to melt. Cut into wedges to serve. Serves 4.

In-a-Hurry Cheesy Strata

This skip-a-step casserole eliminates the overnight standing time of traditional strata.

2 tablespoons chopped green
　　pepper
1 teaspoon water
4 slices white bread
¾ cup shredded Monterey
　　Jack cheese *or* shredded
　　cheddar cheese
　　(3 ounces)
¾ cup milk
½ teaspoon dry mustard
⅛ teaspoon onion powder
2 eggs
2 tablespoons diced pimiento

● In a custard cup combine green pepper and water. Cover with vented plastic wrap. Cook on HIGH for 1 to 2 minutes or till tender, then drain.

● Remove crusts from bread. (Reserve crusts for another use.) Cube bread (you should have about *2 cups*). Place *half* of the cheese into a lightly greased 7-inch pie plate or 1½-quart soufflé dish. Top with bread and ¼ *cup* of remaining cheese. Set aside.

● In a 2-cup measure stir together milk, mustard, and onion powder. Cook, uncovered, on HIGH for 1 to 3 minutes or till *almost* boiling (about 160°), stirring after 1 minute.

● In a medium bowl use a rotary beater to beat eggs. *Gradually* stir in hot milk mixture. Stir in green pepper and pimiento. Pour the egg mixture over bread and cheese in dish. Cook, uncovered, on HIGH for 6 to 8 minutes or till center is puffy and just set, rotating dish a quarter-turn after every 2 minutes.

● Sprinkle with remaining cheese, then let stand for 5 minutes before serving. Makes 2 servings.

Apricot-Bran Muffins
(see recipe, page 16)

**Country
Egg Pie**

Egg Tostada

An "egg-stra" tip: Be sure to prick the yolk and white. Otherwise, during cooking, steam will build and burst the egg.

1 egg
2 tablespoons chunky salsa
½ cup shredded lettuce
2 tablespoons shredded Monterey Jack *or* cheddar cheese (½ ounce)
Tortilla chips *or* corn chips

● Carefully break egg into a custard cup. Prick yolk and white each *3* times with a toothpick. Cover with vented plastic wrap. Cook on HIGH for 40 to 70 seconds or to desired doneness, rotating cup a quarter-turn after every 15 seconds. Let the egg stand, covered, for 2 minutes.

● Meanwhile, place the salsa in another custard cup. Cook, uncovered, on HIGH for 30 to 45 seconds or till heated. To serve, place lettuce on a plate. Using a rubber spatula, remove egg from custard cup and place egg on top of lettuce. Spoon salsa over egg and sprinkle with cheese. Arrange tortilla chips or corn chips around edge of plate. Makes 1 serving.

Cheese and Corn Casseroles

1½ cups frozen whole kernel corn
¼ cup sliced green onion
¼ cup chopped green *or* red sweet pepper
1 tablespoon margarine *or* butter
1 cup shredded American cheese (4 ounces)
½ cup milk
Several dashes bottled hot pepper sauce
3 eggs
1 tablespoon sunflower nuts *or* toasted wheat germ

● In a 1½-quart casserole combine frozen corn, green onion, sweet pepper, and margarine or butter. Cook, covered, on HIGH for 4 to 7 minutes or till tender, stirring after every 2 minutes.

● Stir in cheese, milk, and hot pepper sauce. Cook, uncovered, on HIGH for 3 to 5½ minutes or till bubbly.

● In a medium bowl use a rotary beater to beat eggs. *Gradually* stir in hot corn mixture. Then spoon mixture into three 10-ounce soufflé dishes or custard cups. Cook, uncovered, on HIGH for 4 to 6 minutes or till *almost* set, pushing cooked portions to the center of dishes after every 2 minutes and then rearranging dishes in oven. Remove each dish from oven when almost set. Let stand for 5 minutes, then sprinkle with sunflower nuts or wheat germ before serving. Makes 3 servings.

Beer-Cheese Soup

1 cup shredded American cheese (4 ounces)
2 tablespoons all-purpose flour
1 cup milk
¼ cup beer
1 teaspoon dried parsley flakes

● In a 1-quart casserole combine cheese and flour. Stir in milk, beer, and parsley. Cook, uncovered, on HIGH for 4 to 6 minutes or till slightly thickened and bubbly, stirring after every minute. Then cook, uncovered, on HIGH for 30 seconds more. Serves 2.

Make Now, Microwave Later

Combine the best of two worlds—conventional and microwave cooking—and what do you get? Convenient and delicious make-ahead recipes. Choose from eye-opening breakfasts, totable lunches that go beyond sandwiches, and fresh-tasting dinners you can heat in minutes.

The Chilling Facts

Ensure top-notch last-minute meals from the freezer every time by following these hints:

● **Make Now, Microwave Now:** You've just made a recipe and can't wait to eat some. No problem—just remember the timings for heating an unfrozen portion will be shorter than what the recipe calls for.

● **Freezer wrap-ups:** Prevent freezer burn, or drying and discoloring on the food surface, with proper wrapping. Select moisture- and vaporproof wraps and containers—that means they must keep moisture in and air out. If you plan to cook the food in the container it's frozen in, make sure the container is not only freezer-safe, but also microwave-safe. (See Selecting Microwave Cookware, pages 7–8.)

● **Making Plate Dinners:** Turn leftovers into delicious last-minute meals by placing single portions of cooked meat, gravy, and vegetables into partitioned plates. Wrap the plates individually in freezer plastic bags. Then seal, label, and freeze the dinners for up to 1 month.

To reheat, remove bag. Cover with waxed paper. Cook on HIGH till heated, rotating plate a quarter-turn after every 3 minutes. If you notice that some of the food is hot earlier than other food, then cover that food with a small piece of foil to prevent further cooking. (Check your owner's manual to be sure you can use foil in your oven.)

Toting Your Lunch

Being on the go sometimes means eating lunch away from home. Here's how to keep your take-along meal safe and fresh.

● In the morning, place each lunch serving in an insulated lunch box with a frozen ice pack. Use the ice packs designed for coolers. You can buy these blue plastic ice packs at discount stores, hardware stores, and supermarkets. Freeze the pack overnight so it's frozen solid when you pack your lunch in the morning.

● Keep fruit juices, milk, and canned fruits cold in prechilled insulated vacuum bottles. To prechill the bottle, fill it with the coldest tap water. Cover with the lid and let it stand for 5 minutes. Empty the bottle, then fill it immediately with the cold beverage or fruit.

● Choose fresh fruits that pack well, such as apples, pears, oranges, grapes, bananas, peaches, nectarines, plums, and dark sweet cherries.

● Don't forget to pack the utensils you'll need to heat and eat your lunch. Include a knife, fork, spoon, and paper plate or towels for reheating, as needed. Keep frequently used items in your locker or desk.

● Keep your lunch in a *cool* dry place all morning.

Note: All of the lunch recipes in this chapter can safely be kept in an insulated lunch box with a freezer pack for up to five hours. Any lunch recipe held longer than five hours should be refrigerated.

Morning Stuffed Pockets

¼ cup sliced green onion
1 tablespoon margarine
  or butter
6 eggs
¼ cup milk
1 single-serving-size envelope
  instant cream of chicken
  or cream of mushroom
  soup mix
⅛ teaspoon pepper
½ of an 8-ounce package
  (5 links) brown-and-serve
  sausage links, sliced
2 tablespoons diced
  pimiento
½ cup shredded American
  cheese (2 ounces)
2 large pita bread rounds,
  halved crosswise

● In a 1½-quart casserole combine onion and margarine or butter. Micro-cook, uncovered, on HIGH for 1½ to 2 minutes or till onion is tender.

● In a bowl use a rotary beater to beat eggs, milk, soup mix, and pepper together. Stir in sausage and pimiento. Stir egg mixture into onion mixture. Micro-cook, uncovered, on HIGH for 6 to 7 minutes or till eggs are *almost* set, pushing cooked portions to center of casserole after every 2 mintues. Add cheese, then toss lightly till combined. Let stand till cool.

● To assemble, spoon egg mixture into pita pockets. Then place stuffed pitas in individual freezer plastic bags. Seal, label, and freeze for up to 1 month. Makes 4 servings.

To reheat: Remove plastic bag. Loosely wrap stuffed pita in a paper towel, then place on a plate. Micro-cook 1 frozen portion on HIGH for 2½ to 3 minutes or just till heated, rotating plate a quarter-turn after every minute. (For 2 frozen portions: micro-cook, loosely wrapped, on HIGH for 5 to 7 minutes or just till heated, turning the stuffed pitas over after every 2 minutes and then rotating plate a quarter-turn.)

Mini-Breakfast Cakes

1 cup all-purpose flour
1 cup quick-cooking rolled
  oats
¾ teaspoon baking powder
¾ teaspoon baking soda
1 beaten egg
¾ cup milk
⅔ cup packed brown sugar
⅓ cup cooking oil
½ cup chopped walnuts,
  miniature semisweet
  chocolate pieces, raisins,
  or mixed dried fruit bits
Granola, slightly crushed
  (optional)
Breakfast Butter (see tip,
  page 40) (optional)

● In a medium mixing bowl combine flour, oats, baking powder, and baking soda. In a small mixing bowl combine egg, milk, brown sugar, and oil. Add egg mixture to flour mixture, then stir just till moistened. Fold in nuts, chocolate pieces, raisins, or fruit. Transfer to a tightly covered container. Label and refrigerate for up to 1 week. Makes 12.

To micro-cook: Stir batter. Line 6-ounce custard cups or a microwave-safe muffin pan with paper bake cups. For *each* cake, spoon about *3 tablespoons* batter into a prepared cup. If desired, sprinkle with a *scant teaspoon* granola.
● If using custard cups, arrange them in a circle. Micro-cook *6* cakes, uncovered, on HIGH for 2½ to 4½ minutes or till cakes have a crumb texture when the surfaces are scratched with a toothpick, rearranging custard cups or rotating muffin pan a quarter-turn after every minute. If using custard cups, remove each cup from oven when done. (For *4* cakes, micro-cook 1½ to 3 minutes; for *2* cakes, micro-cook 1 to 2 minutes; for *1* cake, micro-cook 30 to 60 seconds.) Remove cakes from cups or pan. If desired, serve with Breakfast Butter.

Fruit and Bulgur Porridge

½ cup bulgur
⅓ cup mixed dried fruit bits
   or raisins
¼ cup quick-cooking rolled
   oats
¼ teaspoon salt
1½ cups water
1 tablespoon molasses
   Milk

● For cereal mixture, in a 1-quart casserole stir together bulgur, fruit bits or raisins, oats, and salt. Then stir in water and molasses. Cover, label, and refrigerate mixture overnight or for up to 3 days. Makes 2 servings.

To micro-cook: Stir mixture. For 1 serving: place *1 cup* mixture in a large cereal bowl. Cover with vented plastic wrap. Micro-cook on HIGH for 4 to 6 minutes or till heated and liquid is absorbed, stirring after 3 minutes. (For 2 servings: micro-cook *all* of the mixture, covered, on HIGH for 6 to 7 minutes or till heated and liquid is absorbed, stirring after every 2 minutes.) Serve with milk.

Apple-Cinnamon Oatmeal Mix

Cereal, fruit, and milk makes this a complete one-dish breakfast.

2 cups quick-cooking rolled
   oats
½ cup nonfat dry milk powder
¼ cup snipped dried apples *or*
   raisins
2 tablespoons brown sugar
½ teaspoon ground cinnamon
   or apple pie spice
¼ teaspoon salt

● For cereal mixture, in an airtight storage container combine the oats, dry milk powder, apples or raisins, brown sugar, cinnamon or apple pie spice, and salt. Cover, label, and store at room temperature for up to 3 months. Makes 5 servings.

To micro-cook: Shake the container to distribute ingredients. For 1 serving: in a large cereal bowl stir together ⅔ cup *hot water* and ½ *cup* cereal mixture. Micro-cook, uncovered, on HIGH for 1 to 2 minutes or till mixture begins to thicken, stirring after 1 minute. (For 2 servings: in a 1-quart casserole stir together 1⅓ cups *hot water* and *1 cup* cereal mixture. Micro-cook, uncovered, on HIGH for 3 to 4 minutes or till mixture begins to thicken, stirring after every minute.) Let stand, covered, for 1 minute. Then stir before serving.

Breakfast Butter

Spread a little sweetness onto reheated frozen pancakes, French toast, or waffles (see chart, page 72), or Apricot-Bran Muffins or Mini-Breakfast Cakes (see recipes, pages 16 and 39) with this butter spread:

   In a small covered container stir together ½ cup softened *butter or margarine* (see Micro-Cooking Tips, page 77) and 2 tablespoons *honey, or maple or maple-flavored syrup*. Then store the spread in the covered container in the refrigerator until you're ready to use it.

Bacon 'n' Cheese Burgers

With this easy-to-pack burger, you can have fast food for lunch without leaving the office.

¼ cup quick-cooking rice
¼ cup water
½ cup shredded cheddar,
   Monterey Jack, Swiss,
   or mozzarella cheese
   (2 ounces)
4 slices bacon, crisp-cooked,
   drained, and crumbled
   (see chart, page 70)
1 beaten egg
¼ cup fine dry bread crumbs
2 small green onions, thinly
   sliced
2 tablespoons catsup
1 tablespoon prepared
   mustard
1 pound lean ground beef
4 hamburger buns, split
   and toasted

● In a small bowl combine rice and water. Cover with vented plastic wrap. Micro-cook on HIGH for 1½ to 3½ minutes or till boiling. Then let stand, covered, about 5 minutes or till water is absorbed. Add cheese and bacon. Gently toss, then set aside.

● Meanwhile, in a medium mixing bowl stir together egg, bread crumbs, green onion, catsup, and mustard. Add ground beef and mix well. Shape mixture into *eight* ¼-inch-thick patties.

● To stuff burgers, place *half* of the patties on a piece of waxed paper. Then place cheese mixture on top of the patties, spreading to within ½ inch of the edges. Place remaining patties on top, then press edges together to seal.

● Transfer the *4* stuffed burgers to an 8x8x2-inch baking dish. (*Or,* for a very small cavity oven, transfer *2* burgers to a medium-size dinner plate.) Cover with waxed paper. Micro-cook on HIGH for 4 minutes. Turn patties over so outside edges face center of dish and then rotate the dish a half-turn. For 4 burgers: micro-cook, covered, on HIGH for 6 to 8 minutes more or till no longer pink, rotating dish a half-turn after 3 minutes. (For 2 burgers: micro-cook, covered, on HIGH for 3 to 5 minutes more or till done, rotating plate a half-turn after 2 minutes. Then repeat micro-cooking the remaining 2 burgers.)

● Transfer burgers to paper towels to drain and cool slightly. Then place burgers in individual freezer plastic bags. Seal, label, and freeze for up to 1 month. Makes 4 servings.

To tote and reheat: In the morning, place a toasted bun in a plastic bag, then seal. Pack bun, 1 frozen burger, and a paper plate in an insulated lunch box with a frozen ice pack.
● To reheat, remove the plastic bag from burger. Place burger on the paper plate. Micro-cook, uncovered, on HIGH for 2 to 3 minutes or till heated, rotating plate a half-turn after 1 minute. Serve burger in the bun.

Macaroni Minestrone

Macaroni Minestrone

Just cook the macaroni. Then, stir the ingredients together and freeze—it's that simple to have a homemade, totable soup.

1½ cups warm water
1 teaspoon instant beef
    bouillon granules
1 15-ounce can navy beans
1 cup frozen mixed
    vegetables
1 cup cooked elbow macaroni
    (about ⅓ cup, uncooked)
1 8-ounce can tomato sauce
1 3½-ounce package sliced
    pepperoni, halved
1 teaspoon sugar
½ teaspoon dried basil,
    crushed
¼ teaspoon dried oregano,
    crushed

● For soup, in a large mixing bowl stir together water and bouillon granules till dissolved. Then stir in *undrained* beans, mixed vegetables, cooked macaroni, tomato sauce, pepperoni, sugar, basil, and oregano.

● Spoon soup into four 2-cup containers, leaving about ½ inch of space below the rim (headspace) of the containers. Cover with tight-fitting lids. Label and freeze for up to 3 months. Serves 4.

To tote and heat: In the morning, pack 1 frozen portion and a spoon in an insulated lunch box.
● To heat, vent the lid on the container. Micro-cook on HIGH for 6 to 8 minutes or till heated, stirring after 3 minutes.

Calzones

Add pizzazz to your lunch with a zesty pizza in a bun.

12 ounces lean ground beef
¼ cup chopped onion
¼ cup chopped green pepper
2 cloves garlic, minced, *or*
    ¼ teaspoon garlic powder
½ cup pizza sauce
3 tablespoons grated
    Parmesan cheese
½ teaspoon dried Italian
    seasoning
1 10-ounce package
    refrigerated pizza dough

● For filling, in a 1-quart casserole combine loose ground beef, onion, green pepper, and garlic. Micro-cook, covered, on HIGH for 5 to 7 minutes or till no longer pink, stirring after every 3 minutes. Drain off juices, then stir in pizza sauce, Parmesan cheese, and Italian seasoning.

● To assemble calzones, unroll refrigerated dough. Pat dough into a 12x10-inch rectangle, then cut rectangle into *four* 6x5-inch rectangles. Spoon filling onto *half* of *each* rectangle to within ½ inch of edges. Fold plain dough half over top of filling. Pinch edges to seal. Place on a greased baking sheet. Cut a small slit in the top of each for steam to escape. Bake in a 425° oven for 8 to 10 minutes or till golden. Transfer calzones from the baking sheet to a wire rack. Cool. Then place calzones in individual freezer plastic bags. Seal, label, and freeze for up to 3 months. Makes 4 servings.

To tote and reheat: In the morning, pack 1 frozen calzone and a paper towel in an insulated lunch box with a frozen ice pack.
● To reheat, remove the plastic bag, then loosely wrap the calzone in the paper towel. Micro-cook on HIGH for 1 to 3 minutes or till calzone is heated.

43

Cashew-Ginger Chicken

Add quick-cooking rice or chow mein noodles to quickly round out this meal.

1 10-ounce jar mandarin orange sauce *or* one 9-ounce jar sweet-and-sour sauce
2 green onions, sliced
¼ teaspoon ground ginger
⅛ teaspoon crushed red pepper
1 pound boned skinless chicken breast halves, cut into bite-size strips
2 small carrots, thinly bias sliced
1 10-ounce package frozen cauliflower
¼ cup finely chopped red sweet pepper
¼ cup cashews

● For sauce, in a bowl stir together mandarin orange or sweet-and-sour sauce, onions, ginger, and crushed red pepper. Set aside. In a 1½-quart casserole combine chicken and carrots. Micro-cook, covered, on HIGH for 6 to 10 minutes or till chicken is no longer pink, stirring after every 3 minutes. Drain.

● If necessary, cut large cauliflower pieces into bite-size pieces. Add frozen cauliflower and red sweet pepper to chicken mixture. Pour sauce over mixture, then gently toss till coated. Spoon mixture into 4 individual casseroles. Cover with tight-fitting lids, or with plastic wrap, then foil. Label and freeze for up to 6 weeks. Makes 4 servings.

To reheat: If necessary, remove foil. Vent plastic wrap or lid. Micro-cook 1 frozen portion on HIGH for 5 to 7 minutes or till heated, stirring after 3 minutes. (For 2 frozen portions: micro-cook, covered, on HIGH for 10 to 12 minutes or till heated, stirring after 5 minutes.) Top *each* with *1 tablespoon* cashews.

Make-Ahead Lasagna

4 no-boil lasagna noodles
8 ounces bulk Italian sausage
1 15½-ounce jar chunk-style meatless spaghetti sauce
1 cup ricotta cheese
½ cup grated Parmesan cheese
¾ cup shredded mozzarella cheese (3 ounces)

● Place noodles in a baking dish. Pour in enough *warm water* to cover noodles. Let stand for 5 minutes, then drain well. Cut *each* noodle crosswise in half; set aside. For meat mixture, place loose ground sausage in a 1-quart casserole. Micro-cook, covered, on HIGH for 5 to 6 minutes or till done, stirring after 3 minutes. Drain; stir in spaghetti sauce. For cheese mixture, in a bowl combine ricotta cheese and *half* of Parmesan cheese.

● To assemble lasagnas, use 4 individual casseroles. Spread *2 tablespoons* of meat mixture in bottom of *each* casserole. Place *half* of the noodle halves in casseroles. Top with *half* of remaining meat mixture, and *half* of mozzarella cheese. Repeat layers with remaining noodles, all of the ricotta cheese mixture, remaining meat mixture, and remaining mozzarella cheese. Cover with tight-fitting lids, or with plastic wrap, then foil. Label and freeze for up for up to 3 months. Makes 4 servings.

To reheat: If necessary, remove foil. Vent wrap or lid. Micro-cook 1 frozen portion on HIGH for 7 to 10 minutes or till heated, rotating casserole a quarter-turn after 4 minutes. (For 2 frozen portions: micro-cook, covered, on HIGH for 13 to 16 minutes or till heated, rotating a quarter-turn after 7 minutes.) Sprinkle *each* with *1 tablespoon* of remaining Parmesan cheese.

Cashew-Ginger Chicken

Spinach-Stuffed Chicken Breasts

A last-minute dinner guest? Here's a frozen dinner grand enough for company.

1 10-ounce package frozen
   chopped spinach, thawed
   and drained well*
1 medium carrot, shredded
   (½ cup)
2 tablespoons finely chopped
   onion
2 tablespoons grated
   Parmesan cheese
1 10-ounce package frozen
   long grain and wild rice
   mix
1¼ cups milk
1 tablespoon cornstarch
½ of an 8-ounce container
   soft-style cream cheese
   with chives and onion
2 tablespoons dry white wine
4 boned skinless chicken
   breast halves (about
   1 pound total)
   Salt
   Snipped chives (optional)

● For filling, in a medium mixing bowl combine spinach, carrot, and onion. Stir in Parmesan cheese, then set aside.

● Cut a small slit in the pouch of rice. Then place the pouch on a plate and micro-cook on HIGH for 1½ to 3 minutes or till *partially* thawed. Unwrap rice, then cut rice block into *4* equal pieces. Set rice aside.

● For sauce, in a 4-cup measure combine milk and cornstarch. Micro-cook, uncovered, on HIGH for 5 to 10 minutes or till thickened and bubbly, stirring after every minute. Stir in cream cheese till melted, then stir in wine and set aside.

● For chicken rolls, place *1* chicken piece, boned side up, between *2* pieces of clear plastic wrap. Working from the center to edges, pound lightly with the flat side of a meat mallet to form a rectangle about ⅛ inch thick. Remove plastic wrap. Sprinkle lightly with salt. Repeat with remaining chicken pieces. Spoon about *¼ cup* spinach mixture on top of each piece of chicken. Fold in sides and bottoms, then roll up jelly-roll style. Place rolls, seam side down, in a shallow baking dish. Cover with vented plastic wrap. Micro-cook on HIGH for 6 minutes. Then rearrange rolls by moving the outside rolls to the center of the dish. Micro-cook, covered, on HIGH for 2 to 4 minutes or till chicken is no longer pink.

● To assemble, use 4 individual oblong casseroles. Place *1* chicken roll in half of *each* casserole and *1* piece of rice in the other half of each casserole. Pour sauce over chicken rolls. Cover with tight-fitting lids, or with plastic wrap, then foil. Label and freeze for up to 4 months. Makes 4 servings.

To reheat: If necessary, remove foil. Vent plastic wrap or lid. Micro-cook 1 frozen portion on HIGH for 12 to 17 minutes or till heated, rotating casserole a half-turn after 7 minutes. (For 2 frozen portions: micro-cook, covered, on HIGH for 14 to 22 minutes or till heated, rotating casseroles a half-turn after 10 minutes.) If desired, garnish with snipped chives.

*To micro-thaw spinach, remove spinach from package. Place spinach in a 1-quart casserole. Cook, uncovered, on HIGH for 4 to 7 minutes or till thawed, breaking up block after 3 minutes. Squeeze excess liquid from spinach.

No-Fuss Vegetables

Micro-cooking vegetables—
it's fast and easy, and holds
in vitamins and minerals while
preserving the vegetables'
fresh colors and textures. With
so many benefits, why cook
vegetables any other way?

Cooking Fresh Vegetables

Use the charts on the next few pages as a quick reference when you want to micro-cook vegetables.

Most of the timings on these charts are for two or three servings. To cook double the amount of the vegetable listed, add 1½ to 2 minutes to the micro-cooking time.

Avoid uneven cooking by cutting vegetables into uniform-size pieces. Cut the vegetables into ¼-inch-thick slices, ½-inch cubes, 3- to 4-inch lengths, or other small, uniformly sized pieces.

Acorn squash
  One 8-ounce half
  Two 8-ounce halves

Artichokes
  One 10-ounce
  Two 10-ounce

Asparagus cuts
  8 ounces (1½ cups)

Asparagus spears
  8 ounces

Beans (green or wax)
  8 ounces whole or cuts
  (1½ cups)

Broccoli cuts
  8 ounces cuts (2 cups)

Broccoli spears
  8 ounces

Brussels sprouts
  8 ounces (2 cups)

Butternut squash
  One 8-ounce half
  Two 8-ounce halves

Cabbage, shredded
  4 ounces (2 cups)

Power Level & Time	Method
HIGH 6 to 8 minutes 9 to 11 minutes	Wash squash and cut in half. Remove seeds. Place squash, cut sides up, in a baking dish with 2 tablespoons water. Cover with vented plastic wrap. Cook till tender, rearranging once. Drain.
HIGH 6 to 8 minutes 10 to 12 minutes	Wash the artichokes. Then cut off 1 inch from the top of each artichoke and snip off sharp leaf tips. Brush cut edges with lemon juice. Place artichokes in a casserole with 2 tablespoons water. Cook, covered, till a leaf pulls out easily, rearranging once. Drain.
HIGH 6 to 8 minutes	Wash the asparagus and scrape off any scales. Break off woody bases. Then cut into 1-inch pieces. Place asparagus in a casserole with 2 tablespoons water. Cook, covered, till nearly tender, stirring once. Drain.
HIGH 4 to 6 minutes	Wash the asparagus and scrape off any scales. Break off woody bases. Place asparagus in a baking dish with 2 tablespoons water. Cover with vented plastic wrap. Cook, covered, till nearly tender, rearranging once. Drain.
HIGH 12 to 14 minutes	Wash the beans. If desired, cut into 1-inch pieces. Place the beans in a casserole with 2 tablespoons water. Cook, covered, till tender, stirring or rearranging once. Drain.
HIGH 6 to 9 minutes	Wash broccoli. Remove outer leaves. Cut off tough parts of stalks. Then cut into ½-inch pieces. Place in a casserole with 2 tablespoons water. Cook, covered, till nearly tender, stirring once. Drain.
HIGH 6 to 8 minutes	Wash broccoli. Remove outer leaves. Cut off tough parts of stalk. Then cut lengthwise into uniform spears, following the branching lines. Place the broccoli in a baking dish with 2 tablespoons water. Cover with vented plastic wrap. Cook till tender, rearranging once. Drain.
HIGH 4 to 6 minutes	Trim stems from brussels sprouts. Remove any wilted outer leaves and wash. Cut any large sprouts in half to make all of uniform size. Place in a casserole with 2 tablespoons water. Cook, covered, till tender, stirring once. Drain.
HIGH 9 to 11 minutes 12 to 14 minutes	Wash the squash and cut squash in half. Remove seeds from the squash. Place squash, cut sides up, in a baking dish with 2 tablespoons water. Cover with vented plastic wrap. Cook till tender, rearranging once. Drain.
HIGH 7 to 9 minutes	Remove any wilted outer leaves and wash cabbage. Cut head into quarters, then cut out core. Using a long-bladed knife, cut cabbage into coarse ¼-inch-wide shreds. Place in a casserole with 2 tablespoons water. Cook, covered, till nearly tender, stirring once. Drain.

Cooking Fresh Vegetables

To cook frozen vegetables in your low-wattage microwave oven, cook them according to the package's microwave directions. Then, if they are not done, cook them for 1 to 3 minutes more.

Vent microwave-safe plastic wrap by turning back a corner. This will release some of the steam pressure that builds up during cooking, but will still keep enough steam in the dish to speed cooking. (See tip, page 18.)

Food & Amount

Carrots
8 ounces (1½ cups)

Cauliflower flowerets
8 ounces (2 cups)

Corn on the cob
One 7-ounce ear
Two 7-ounce ears

Mushrooms
8 ounces sliced (3 cups)

Parsnips
8 ounces (1½ cups)

Peas, shelled
2 cups

Pepper, sweet
1 medium
2 medium

Potatoes, cubed
2 medium (1½ cups)

Potatoes, whole
One 6- to 8-ounce
Two 6- to 8-ounce

Rutabaga
8 ounces (1⅔ cups)

Spinach
8 ounces (6 cups)

Zucchini
8 ounces (2 cups)

Power Level & Time	Method
HIGH 8 to 10 minutes	Wash, trim, and peel the carrots. Then cut into ¼-inch slices. Place carrots in a casserole with 2 tablespoons water. Cook, covered, till nearly tender, stirring once. Drain.
HIGH 6 to 8 minutes	Wash the cauliflower. Then remove leaves and woody stem. Break cauliflower into flowerets. Place cauliflower flowerets in a casserole with 2 tablespoons water. Cook, covered, till nearly tender, stirring once. Drain.
HIGH 6 to 8 minutes 8 to 10 minutes	Remove the husks from the corn. Scrub the corn with a stiff brush to remove the silks, then rinse. Wrap each ear in waxed paper. Cook till tender, turning ears over once.
HIGH 5 to 7 minutes	Wash the mushrooms. Then cut into ¼-inch-thick slices. Place mushrooms in a casserole with 2 tablespoons margarine or butter. Cook, covered, till tender, stirring once.
HIGH 6 to 8 minutes	Wash, trim, and peel parsnips. Cut into ¼-inch-thick slices. Place parsnips in a casserole with 2 tablespoons water. Cook, covered, till nearly tender, stirring once. Drain.
HIGH 4 to 6 minutes	Rinse the shelled peas. Place peas in a casserole with 2 tablespoons water. Cook, covered, till tender, stirring once. Drain.
HIGH 2 to 2½ minutes 4 to 5 minutes	Wash the peppers and cut in half. Remove seeds. Cut into strips. Place pepper strips in a casserole with 2 tablespoons water. Cook, covered, till nearly tender. Drain.
HIGH 7 to 9 minutes	Peel potatoes. Then cut into 1-inch cubes. Place potatoes in a casserole with 3 tablespoons water. Cook, covered, till tender. Drain.
HIGH 7 to 9 minutes 11 to 13 minutes	Scrub potatoes. Prick several times with a fork. Place on a plate. Cook, uncovered, till tender, rotating plate a quarter-turn once. Then let potatoes stand for 5 minutes to finish cooking.
HIGH 8 to 10 minutes	Wash and peel rutabaga. Cut into ½-inch cubes. Place rutabaga in a casserole with 2 tablespoons water. Cook, covered, till tender, stirring after every 3 minutes. Drain.
HIGH 7 to 9 minutes	Wash spinach. Remove large center veins. Place in a casserole with 2 tablespoons water. Cook, covered, till tender, stirring once. Drain.
HIGH 4 to 6 minutes	Wash zucchini. Then cut into ¼-inch-thick slices. Place zucchini in a casserole with 2 tablespoons water. Cook, covered, till tender, stirring after every 2 minutes. Drain.

Twice-Baked Yams

Company coming for dinner? Cover and chill the stuffed potatoes ahead. Then to heat, micro-cook, uncovered, for 4 to 5 minutes, rotating plate after every 2 minutes.

2 medium yams *or* sweet potatoes (6 to 8 ounces each)
2 tablespoons milk
1 tablespoon margarine *or* butter
1 tablespoon maple-flavored syrup
1 tablespoon chopped pecans *or* walnuts (toasted, if desired—see Micro-Cooking Tips, page 78)

● Scrub potatoes. Prick several times with a fork. Place potatoes on a plate. Cook, uncovered, on HIGH for 11 to 13 minutes or till tender, rotating plate a quarter-turn after 6 minutes. Let stand about 5 minutes or till cool enough to handle.

● Cut a lengthwise slice from top of each potato. Remove pulp from the slice and put pulp into a small mixer bowl. Discard peel. Then scoop pulp from each potato, leaving a ¼-inch-thick shell. Add pulp to mixer bowl. Set potato shells aside.

● Add milk, margarine or butter, and syrup to pulp in bowl. Beat with an electric mixer on low speed till light and fluffy.

● Place potato shells on the plate. Spoon mashed potato into shells. *Or*, use a decorating bag with a large star tip and pipe the potato mixture into shells. Sprinkle with nuts.

● Cook stuffed potatoes, uncovered, on HIGH for 3 to 4 mintues or till heated, rotating plate a quarter-turn after 2 mintues. Makes 2 servings.

Spaghetti Squash with Parmesan Sauce

Serve with grilled salmon for an impressive yet easy dinner.

½ of a 2- to 2½-pound spaghetti squash (halved lengthwise)
½ cup sliced celery
¼ cup chopped onion
1 small carrot, shredded
1 tablespoon margarine *or* butter
1 teaspoon all-purpose flour
¼ teaspoon dry mustard
Dash pepper
½ cup milk
1 slice process Swiss cheese, torn into small pieces (1 ounce)
2 tablespoons grated Parmesan cheese

● Scoop seeds from squash half. Place squash half, cut side down, on a medium-size dinner plate. Cook, uncovered, on HIGH for 10 to 14 minutes or till pulp can just be pierced with a fork, rotating plate a half-turn after 6 minutes. Let stand, cut side down, while preparing sauce.

● For sauce, in a 1-quart casserole combine celery, carrot, onion, and margarine or butter. Cook, covered, on HIGH for 3 to 4 minutes or till onion is tender.

● Stir in flour, mustard, and pepper. Then stir in milk. Cook, uncovered, on HIGH for 1 to 3 minutes or till thickened and bubbly, stirring after every minute. Stir in Swiss and Parmesan cheese till Swiss cheese is melted.

● To serve, use a fork to remove pulp from squash shell by shredding and separating pulp into strands. Pile squash pulp onto a platter. Then spoon sauce over squash. Serves 2 or 3.

Spaghetti Squash
with Parmesan Sauce

Cheese-Sauced Vegetables

Create your own favorite combination: You choose the vegetable and you pick the cheese.

1 tablespoon margarine
   or butter
1 tablespoon all-purpose
   flour
½ cup milk
½ cup shredded cheddar,
   Swiss, sharp American,
   Havarti, Monterey Jack,
   Muenster, *or* brick
   cheese (2 ounces)
4 servings hot cooked
   vegetables (see charts,
   pages 48–51)

● For sauce, place margarine or butter in a 2-cup measure. Cook, uncovered, on HIGH for 20 to 40 seconds or till melted. Stir in flour, dash *salt,* and dash *pepper.* Then stir in milk. Cook, uncovered, on HIGH for 2 to 4 minutes or till thickened and bubbly, stirring after one minute and then after every 30 seconds. Stir in cheese. If necessary, cook, uncovered, on HIGH for 30 seconds to 1 minute more or till cheese is melted.

● To serve, arrange cooked vegetables on a platter. Then pour sauce over vegetables. Makes 4 servngs.

Flavored-Buttered Vegetables

1 tablespoon butter
   or margarine
⅛ teaspoon garlic powder,
   dried dillweed, *or* dried
   basil, crushed
   Dash pepper
2 servings hot cooked
   vegetables (see charts,
   pages 48–51)

● In a custard cup combine butter or margarine; garlic powder, dill, or basil; and pepper. Cook, uncovered, on HIGH for 20 to 40 seconds or till melted.

● To serve, place cooked vegetables in a serving dish. Drizzle butter mixture over vegetables. Then lightly toss till coated. Makes 2 servings.

Baked Beans Supreme

½ cup chopped onion
½ cup chopped celery
   or green pepper
1 small clove garlic, minced,
   or ⅛ teaspoon garlic
   powder
1 tablespoon water
1 15-ounce can butter
   beans, drained
1 8-ounce can red kidney
   beans, drained
½ cup bottled barbecue sauce
1 tablespoon molasses
⅛ teaspoon pepper

● In a 1-quart casserole combine onion, celery or green pepper, garlic, and water. Cook, covered, on HIGH for 5 to 6 minutes or till vegetables are tender.

● Stir in butter beans, kidney beans, barbecue sauce, molasses, and pepper. Cook, covered, on HIGH for 8 to 10 minutes or till heated, stirring after every 4 minutes. Makes 4 to 6 servings.

Short 'n' Sweet Desserts & Candies

Oh, so sweet and oh, so luscious. Indulge in our no-fuss desserts and candies. Try anything from Piña-Colada Upside-Down Cake to Cheese-cake Tarts to Choco-Scotch Crunchies. You'll know you're a success when you hear all of the "Mmms!"

Short 'n' Sweet Dessert & Candy Tips

Dessert Coffees

Top off a great meal with one of these special coffee flavors:

In a 2-cup measure combine ¾ cup *water* and 1 rounded teaspoon *instant coffee crystals*. Cook, uncovered, on HIGH for 2 to 4 minutes or till hot. Stir till combined, then pour coffee into a mug. Stir in *one* of the flavorings at right. If desired, top with *pressurized whipped dairy dessert topping* and sprinkle with ground *cinnamon or nutmeg*.

1 tablespoon Irish whiskey *plus* 2 teaspoons brown sugar
1 tablespoon Amaretto
2 teaspoons crème de cacao *plus* 2 teaspoons brandy
1 tablespoon coffee liqueur

Storing Candy

Whether you're storing an assortment of candies for holiday guests or keeping just one batch on hand to satisfy your own sweet tooth, candies will stay fresh longer if you store them properly.

Keep most candies tightly covered in a cool dry place for up to three weeks. Soft chocolate candies, however, will need to be stored in the refrigerator.

For longer storage, you can freeze candies such as Chocolate 'Tater Fudge, Choco-Scotch Crunchies, or Rocky Road (see recipes, pages 61 and 62). Remove the candy from the pan or baking sheet. Then place it in an airtight freezer bag or container. Seal, label, and freeze for up to 6 months.

To thaw the candy, remove it from the freezer and let it stand several hours to warm to room temperature before opening or unwrapping it. This will prevent moisture from collecting on the surface of the candy and causing white speckles or gray streaks on the chocolate.

Piña-Colada Upside-Down Cake

Micro-bake the cake in the pan that comes with the cake mix.

1 8.6-ounce package
   microwave yellow
   cake mix
1 8-ounce can crushed
   pineapple (juice pack),
   well drained
⅓ cup coconut (toasted,
   if desired)
⅓ cup cream of coconut
2 tablespoons rum
   Frozen whipped dessert
   topping, thawed (see
   chart, page 68) (optional)

● Grease the reusable, 7-inch microwave-safe cake pan. Then set the cake pan aside.

● For pineapple-coconut topping, in a small mixing bowl stir together pineapple, coconut, cream of coconut, and rum. Spoon mixture evenly into the prepared cake pan. Cook, uncovered, on HIGH for 3 to 5 minutes or till hot and bubbly, stirring after 2 minutes. (Center may not get bubbly.) Then spread topping evenly in pan.

● Meanwhile, prepare the cake batter according to package directions. Then spoon batter evenly over hot topping. Cook, uncovered, on HIGH for 6 to 8 minutes or till cake has a crumb texture when surface is scratched with a toothpick, rotating pan a half-turn after 3 minutes.

● Let cake stand in its pan on a wire rack for 5 minutes. Then invert cake onto a plate. If necessary, spoon any pineapple-coconut topping left in the pan onto the top of the cake. If desired, serve warm with whipped topping. Serves 6 to 8.

Chocolate Chip Wedges

Satisfy a sudden chocolate craving with these speedy wedges.

1 tablespoon finely crushed
   graham cracker crumbs,
   toasted wheat germ, *or*
   ground nuts
¼ cup margarine *or* butter,
   softened (see Micro-
   Cooking Tips, page 77)
⅓ cup packed brown sugar
¼ teaspoon vanilla
1 egg yolk
½ cup all-purpose flour
¼ teaspoon baking soda
⅓ cup milk
¼ cup semisweet chocolate
   pieces, peanut butter-
   flavored pieces, *or*
   chopped pitted dates
¼ cup chopped nuts
   Ice cream (optional)
   Chocolate ice-cream
   topping (optional)

● Grease a 7-inch pie plate or a 1½-quart casserole. Then sprinkle bottom and sides of dish with graham cracker crumbs, wheat germ, or ground nuts. Set dish aside.

● For batter, in a medium mixing bowl using a wooden spoon combine margarine or butter, brown sugar, and vanilla. Beat in egg yolk. In a small mixing bowl stir together flour and baking soda. Then stir flour mixture and milk into margarine mixture. Spread batter in the prepared dish.

● Sprinkle with chocolate or flavored pieces or dates and chopped nuts. Cook, uncovered, on HIGH for 5 to 7 minutes or till surface is no longer wet and springs back when touched, rotating dish a quarter-turn after every minute. *Do not overcook.* (A few areas on the surface will remain moist, but those areas should only be about ⅛ inch deep.) Cool thoroughly.

● To serve, cut into wedges. If desired, top with ice cream and chocolate topping. Makes 4 servings.

Baked Apple

Dining alone? Here's a single-serving apple dessert filled with fruit.

2 tablespoons chopped
    walnuts *or* pecans
1 tablespoon raisins,
    currants, chopped pitted
    dates, *or* mixed dried
    fruit bits
1 tablespoon brown sugar
    Dash ground cinnamon
1 medium cooking apple
    (6 to 7 ounces)
    Lemon juice
1 teaspoon water

● For filling, in a custard cup combine nuts; raisins, currants, dates or fruit bits; brown sugar; and cinnamon. Set aside.

● Core apple and peel off a strip around top. Brush peeled portion of apple with lemon juice. Place apple and the water in a 10-ounce custard cup. Then spoon filling into apples. Cover with vented plastic wrap.

● Cook on HIGH for 2½ to 6 minutes or till tender, rotating cup a half-turn after every 2 minutes. Serve warm or chilled. Before serving, spoon the liquid over the apple. Makes 1 serving.

Caramel-Apple Crunch

The butterscotch pudding mix gives the fruit a rich caramel coating.

3 medium cooking apples *or*
    pears, peeled, cored, and
    thinly sliced (about
    3 cups)
1 tablespoon water
½ of a 4-serving-size package
    (about ¼ cup) *regular*
    butterscotch pudding
    mix
½ cup granola
    Light cream, whipped
    cream, *or* ice cream

● In a 1½-quart casserole stir together apples or pears and water till fruit is wet. Then sprinkle with dry pudding mix and toss till coated. Cook, covered, on HIGH for 6 to 8 minutes or till tender, stirring after every 3 minutes.

● Gently stir fruit to coat evenly. If desired, stir in an additional 1 to 2 tablespoons *water* to make fruit desired consistency. Sprinkle with granola. Serve warm with light cream, whipped cream, or ice cream. Makes 4 servings.

Ice Cream with Hot-Fudge Sauce

Our food editors rated this fudgy sauce as "a number-one choice."

4 squares (4 ounces)
    semisweet chocolate,
    cut up
⅓ cup whipping cream
3 tablespoons sugar
    Ice cream

● In a 2-cup measure or a small bowl combine chocolate, cream, and sugar. Cook, uncovered, on HIGH for 2 to 3 minutes or till boiling and chocolate and sugar become smooth when stirred, stirring after every minute. Then stir till well blended and creamy looking. Serve warm over ice cream. Transfer any remaining sauce to a tightly covered container. Label and refrigerate. Makes ¾ cup.

To reheat: Place ½ *cup* sauce in a 1-cup measure. Cook, uncovered, on HIGH 1½ to 2 minutes or till heated, stirring once.

Candy-Dipped Fruit
(see recipe, page 61)

**Ice Cream with
Hot-Fudge Sauce**

Very Berry Ice-Cream Topping

A versatile topping that's also great on waffles, pancakes, or pound cake.

1 to 2 teaspoons sugar
1 teaspoon cornstarch
2 tablespoons orange juice
     or rosé wine
½ cup loose-pack frozen
     unsweetened red *or*
     black raspberries
     Vanilla ice cream

● In a 2-cup measure combine sugar and cornstarch, then stir in orange juice or wine. Add frozen berries.

● Cook, uncovered, on HIGH for 2 to 4 minutes or till bubbly, stirring after every minute. Serve the warm berry topping over ice cream. Makes ⅓ cup.

Cheesecake Tarts

For Rum-Flavored Cheesecake Tarts: substitute ½ teaspoon rum flavoring for the lemon peel.

1 8-ounce package cream
     cheese
1 3-ounce package custard
     dessert mix
⅔ cup milk
½ teaspoon grated
     lemon peel
1 4-ounce package (6)
     graham cracker tart
     shells
     Chocolate curls, toasted
     coconut, *or* toasted nuts
     (see Micro-Cooking Tips,
     page 78)

● Place unwrapped cream cheese in a medium bowl. Cook, uncovered, on HIGH for 45 seconds to 1½ minutes or till softened, rotating bowl a half-turn after 30 seconds. Set cream cheese aside.

● Place custard mix in a 1-quart casserole. Stir in milk. Cook, uncovered, on HIGH for 3 to 5 minutes or till boiling, stirring after every minute. *Gradually* stir the custard mixture into softened cream cheese in bowl. Then stir in lemon peel. Spoon about *¼ cup* mixture into *each* tart shell. Cover with clear plastic wrap. Chill for at least 1 hour or till firm. Store in refrigerator for up to 2 days.*

● To serve, garnish with chocolate curls, toasted coconut, or toasted nuts. Makes 6 servings.

*For longer storage, after tarts are firm, place them in a tightly covered container. Label and freeze for up to 4 months. To thaw, remove foil pan from tart. Place on a plate. Cook 1 frozen tart, uncovered, on DEFROST for 45 to 60 seconds or till edges are *just* soft and center is icy. (For 2 frozen tarts: cook, uncovered, on DEFROST for 2 to 2½ minutes or till partially thawed.) Then let stand about 5 minutes or till thawed. Serve as above.

Candy-Dipped Fruit

For a fast festive gift, put the Candy-Dipped Pretzels into a tissue-lined, decorative tin. (Candy-Dipped Cherries are pictured on page 59.)

2 to 2½ cups maraschino
    cherries with stems,
    fresh dark sweet
    cherries with stems,
    fresh strawberries,
    and/or dried fruit
6 ounces (1 cup) semisweet
    chocolate pieces
    or vanilla-flavored
    confectioner's coating,
    cut up
1 tablespoon shortening
¾ to 1 cup very finely
    chopped pecans *or*
    almonds (optional)

● Place cherries and strawberries on paper towels to *drain thoroughly.* Line a baking sheet with waxed paper, then set baking sheet aside. Place chocolate pieces or confectioner's coating and shortening in a 1-quart casserole or bowl. Cook, uncovered, on HIGH for 2 to 4 minutes or just till chocolate becomes smooth when stirred, stirring after every minute.

● To dip fruit, use your fingers to hold fruit by one end. Dip fruit halfway up in the melted chocolate. Let excess chocolate drip off. If desired, dip into chopped nuts. Place on the prepared baking sheet. Chill about 20 minutes or till firm. Serve dipped fruit the same day it is dipped. Makes 6 to 8 servings.

Candy-Dipped Pretzels: Prepare the Candy-Dipped Fruit as directed above, *except* substitute 2 to 2½ cups bite-size *twisted pretzels or* bite-size *rich round crackers* for the fruit. Omit chopped nuts. Store dipped pretzels or crackers in a tightly covered container in a cool place for up to 3 weeks.

Chocolate Tater Fudge

Psst. . . . Stir in the secret ingredients of peanut butter and mashed potatoes for a smooth and creamy fudge.

1 small potato (about
    5 ounces), peeled
    and cut up
2 tablespoons water
1 to 2 tablespoons milk
½ cup semisweet chocolate
    pieces
½ cup peanut butter
½ teaspoon vanilla
1½ cups sifted powdered sugar
    (about 6 ounces)
½ cup finely chopped peanuts

● In a 1-quart casserole combine potato and water. Cook, covered, on HIGH for 5 to 7 minutes or till tender, stirring after 3 minutes. Drain, then mash potato with enough of the milk to make it fluffy. (You should have ⅓ cup mashed potato.) Set mashed potato aside. Wash and dry casserole.

● Meanwhile, line an 8x4x2-inch loaf pan with foil, extending foil over edges of pan. Butter the foil, then set pan aside.

● Place chocolate pieces in the casserole. Cook, uncovered, on HIGH for 1 to 2 minutes or just till chocolate becomes smooth when stirred, stirring after 30 seconds.

● Stir potato, peanut butter, and vanilla into chocolate. Stir in powdered sugar (if necessary, use your hands to mix in the last ¼ cup sugar). Stir in *half* of the peanuts. Turn into the prepared pan. Press down evenly. Sprinkle with remaining peanuts, then press peanuts slightly into fudge. Chill till firm. When firm, use the foil to lift fudge out of pan. Cut into 1-inch pieces. Store in a tightly covered container in a cool, dry place. Makes 32 pieces.

Choco-Scotch Crunchies

For Fruit 'n' Nut Clusters: omit the noodles and marshmallows, and stir the chocolate mixture into 2 cups of peanuts or cashews and 1½ cups of raisins.

1 6-ounce package (1 cup) semisweet chocolate pieces
1 6-ounce package (1 cup) butterscotch pieces
1⅔ cups chow mein noodles
1 cup cocktail peanuts *or* cashews
1 cup tiny marshmallows

● Line a baking sheet with waxed paper, then set it aside. In a 1-quart casserole or bowl combine chocolate and butterscotch pieces. Cook, uncovered, on HIGH for 2 to 3 minutes or just till mixture becomes smooth when stirred, stirring after 1 minute. Meanwhile, in a large mixing bowl combine chow mein noodles, nuts, and marshmallows.

● Pour chocolate mixture over noodle mixture in bowl. Stir till well coated. Drop mixture from a teaspoon onto the prepared baking sheet. Chill till firm. When firm, store candy in a tightly covered container in the refrigerator. Makes 36 pieces.

Malted-Milk Candies

8 ounces bar milk chocolate *or* vanilla-flavored confectioner's coating, cut up
1 4-ounce container frozen whipped dessert topping, thawed (see chart, page 68)
½ cup finely crushed vanilla *or* chocolate wafers
3 tablespoons instant malted milk powder

● Place chocolate or coating in a 1-quart casserole or bowl. Cook, uncovered, on HIGH for 1 to 2½ minutes or just till the chocolate becomes smooth when stirred, stirring after 1 minute. Then cool about 20 minutes or to room temperature.

● Fold thawed dessert topping, *half* of the crushed wafers, and malted milk powder into chocolate in casserole. (Mixture will become thick.) Then cover and chill for at least 1 hour. Form mixture into 1-inch balls and roll in the remaining crumbs. Chill the candy thoroughly. Then store in a tightly covered container in the refrigerator. Makes about 24 pieces.

Rocky Road

An old-time favorite made easy in the microwave.

2 8-ounce bars milk chocolate, cut up
3 cups plain *or* flavored tiny marshmallows
¾ cup coarsely chopped walnuts

● Line a 9x9x2-inch baking pan with foil, extending foil over edges of pan. Butter the foil, then set pan aside. Place chocolate in a 1½-quart casserole or bowl. Cook, uncovered, on HIGH for 2 to 3 minutes or just till the chocolate becomes smooth when stirred, stirring after 1 minute. Stir in marshmallows and nuts.

● Spread the candy into the prepared pan. Chill till firm. When firm, use the foil to lift candy out of the pan. Cut into 1-inch pieces. Store candy in a tightly covered container in the refrigerator. Makes 81 pieces.

Special
Helps

Chock-full of nifty micro-
cooking tips and timings for
defrosting, heating, and cooking
convenience foods, this chapter
offers a complete easy-to-use
reference guide to help you get
the most out of your low-wattage
microwave oven.

Defrosting Meats and Poultry

■ Forgot to thaw something for dinner? Don't worry. The charts on the following four pages will help solve that problem.

Unwrap the frozen meat, poultry, fish, or seafood. Then place it in a single layer in a shallow baking dish to catch the drippings. Cover with vented plastic wrap. After *half* of the defrosting time, re-arrange, separate pieces, turn food over, or break up ground meats.

At the end of the defrosting time, some ice crystals should remain in the center of the pieces. Finish defrosting by allowing the food to stand, covered, until it is completely thawed.

■ If corners begin to cook during defrosting, protect them with small pieces of foil. The strips of foil will shield the corners from micro-waves so they won't defrost faster than the center. (Check your owner's manual to make sure you can use foil in your oven.)

Food & Amount

Meats
Bacon, sliced
  per pound

Cubes, ¾ inch
  per pound

Frankfurters
  per pound

Ground meat *or* bulk sausage
  per pound

Patties, ¾ inch thick
  One 4-ounce patty
  Two 4-ounce patties

Roasts*
  per pound

Poultry
Broiler-fryer chicken, cut up
  one 2½- to 3-pound bird

Broiler-fryer chicken, whole
  one 2½- to 3-pound bird

Chicken breast halves, boned and skinned, *or* turkey tenderloin steaks
  Two 4-ounce pieces
  Four 4-ounce pieces

Chicken breasts, whole
  One 1-pound breast
  Two 1-pound breasts

Chicken drumsticks
  2 drumsticks
  6 drumsticks

Power Level & Time	Method
DEFROST 3½ to 4½ minutes	Place bacon in a baking dish. Cook, covered, till thawed, separating slices once.
DEFROST 6 to 8 minutes	Place meat in a baking dish. Cook, covered, till partially thawed, stirring once. Let stand, covered, about 5 minutes or till thawed.
DEFROST 8 to 10 minutes	Place frankfurters in a baking dish. Cook, covered, till thawed, rearranging once.
DEFROST 6 to 8 minutes	Place the ground meat or sausage in a baking dish. Cook, covered, till thawed, breaking up the ground meat once.
DEFROST 1½ to 3 minutes 5 to 6 minutes	Place patties in a baking dish. Cook, covered, till partially thawed, turning over once so outside edges face center of dish. Let stand, covered, about 5 minutes or till thawed.
DEFROST 10 to 12 minutes	Place roast in a baking dish. Cook, covered, for *half* the cooking time, turning roast over and rotating dish a half-turn once. Let stand, covered, for 10 minutes. Cook, covered, for the remaining time or till partially thawed. Let stand, covered, about 20 minutes or till thawed. (*Do not use this method for rolled or very thick roasts.)
DEFROST 18 to 20 minutes	Place chicken in a baking dish, skin side down, with meaty portions toward edges of dish. Cook, covered, till partially thawed, turning over and rearranging once. Transfer to a bowl of cool water, then let stand 10 minutes or till thawed.
DEFROST 20 to 25 minutes	Place chicken in a baking dish, breast side down. Cook, covered, till partially thawed, turning over once. Transfer to a bowl of cool water, then let stand about 25 minutes or till thawed.
DEFROST 5 to 6 minutes 7 to 10 minutes	Place poultry in a baking dish. Cook, covered, till partially thawed, turning over and rearranging pieces once. Then let stand, covered, about 10 minutes or till thawed.
DEFROST 8 to 10 minutes 13 to 15 minutes	Place chicken in a baking dish, skin side down, with meaty portions toward the edges of dish. Cook, covered, till partially thawed, turning over and rearranging once. Transfer to a bowl of cool water, then let stand 15 minutes or till thawed.
DEFROST 3 to 5 minutes 8 to 10 minutes	In a baking dish arrange drumsticks in a spoke fashion with meaty ends toward edges of dish. Cook, covered, till partially thawed, rotating dish a half-turn once. Transfer to a bowl of cool water, then let stand about 10 minutes or till thawed.

Defrosting Poultry and Fish

Food & Amount

Poultry *(continued)*
Chopped cooked chicken
  per pound (3 cups)

Cornish game hens, whole
  One 1- to 1½-pound bird
  Two 1- to 1½-pound birds

Ground raw turkey
  per pound

Turkey drumstick
  One 1-pound drumstick

Fish
Crab-flavored fish
  One 8-ounce package

Fish fillets *or* steaks
  8 ounces
  1 pound

Fish portions, unbreaded
  ½ of a 12-ounce package
  One 12-ounce package

Seafood
Crabmeat
  One 6-ounce package

Scallops
  8 ounces
  1 pound

Shrimp, deveined, peeled
  8 ounces
  1 pound

Shrimp in shells
  8 ounces
  1 pound

Arrange unevenly shaped pieces so the thicker or meatier parts are toward the edges of the dish. Because foods cook faster near the edges of the dish, the thicker portions will be done at the same time as the thinner portions.

Microwaves can penetrate only ¾ to 2 inches into food. So, to defrost foods evenly, cook till the center yields to moderate fork pressure. Then let stand so the heat from the edges can spread to thaw the center.

Power Level & Time	Method
DEFROST 8 to 10 minutes	Place chicken in a baking dish. Cook, covered, till thawed, stirring once.
DEFROST 12 to 15 minutes 20 to 24 minutes	Place hens, breast side down, in a baking dish. Cook, covered, till partially thawed, turning over once. Transfer to a bowl of cool water, then let stand about 15 minutes or till thawed.
DEFROST 6 to 8 minutes	Place turkey in a baking dish. Cook, covered, till thawed, breaking up meat once. Let stand, covered, about 5 minutes or till thawed.
DEFROST 10 to 12 minutes	Place drumstick in a baking dish. Cook, covered, till partially thawed, turning over and rotating dish a half-turn once. Transfer to a bowl of cool water, then let stand 15 minutes or till thawed.
DEFROST 2 to 3 minutes	Place fish in a baking dish. Cook, covered, till partially thawed, separating pieces and then rotating dish a half-turn once. Let stand, covered, about 5 minutes or till thawed.
DEFROST 5 to 7 minutes 8 to 10 minutes	Place fish in a baking dish. Cook, covered, till partially thawed, turning over and rearranging pieces once. Then let stand, covered, about 10 minutes or till thawed.
DEFROST 4 to 6 minutes 6 to 8 minutes	Place fish in a baking dish. Cook, covered, till partially thawed, separating pieces and turning them over once. Let stand, covered, about 10 minutes or till thawed.
DEFROST 5 to 7 minutes	Place crab in a baking dish. Cook, covered, till partially thawed, rotating dish a half-turn once. Let stand, covered, 5 minutes or till thawed.
DEFROST 3½ to 5 minutes 7 to 10 minutes	Place scallops in a casserole. Cook, covered, till partially thawed, separating scallops and stirring once. Transfer to a bowl of cool water, then let stand about 5 minutes or till thawed.
DEFROST 3 to 5 minutes 8 to 10 minutes	Place shrimp in a casserole. Cook, covered, till partially thawed, separating shrimp and stirring once. Transfer to a bowl of cool water, then let stand about 10 minutes or till thawed.
DEFROST 3 to 4 minutes 7 to 8 minutes	Place shrimp in a casserole. Cook, covered, till partially thawed, separating shrimp and stirring once. Transfer to a bowl of cool water, then let stand about 2 minutes or till thawed.

Defrosting Common Frozen Foods

▬ **W**hether you're thawing a bagel for breakfast or fruit for dessert, your microwave oven can help you speed all types of cooking chores. So when you're in a hurry, make sure this handy chart is close by. In it you'll find defrosting times for many of the frozen foods you use often. (For meat, poultry, and fish defrosting times, see charts on pages 64 and 66.)

▬ **I**f your microwave oven doesn't have a defrost cycle, cook the food on HIGH for *one-third* of the defrost time suggested on the chart. Then let the food stand till it's fully thawed.

▬ **T**o assure even heating, move the food halfway through cooking by stirring or breaking up mixtures, rearranging or turning over large pieces, or rotating the dish.

Food & Amount

Breads
Bagels
  1 bagel
  2 bagels

Bread dough
  One 16-ounce loaf

Bread, sliced
  2 slices
  4 slices

Desserts
Brownie *or* bar cookie, unfrosted
  One 2-inch-square

Cake, frosted single-layer
  One 14-ounce cake

Cake, frosted triple-layer
  One 17- to 20-ounce cake

Cake, pound
  One 10¾-ounce cake

Cheesecake, plain
  1 serving-size wedge
  One 23-ounce whole cheesecake

Dessert topping, whipped dessert
  One 4-ounce container
  One 8-ounce container

Dessert topping, unwhipped
  One 8-ounce carton

Fruits
Fruit, loose-pack
  1 cup

Fruit, syrup-pack
  One 10-ounce carton

Fruit (in pouch)
  One 10-ounce pouch

Power Level & Time	Method
HIGH 30 to 45 seconds 1 to 2 minutes	Place bagels on a paper towel. Cook, uncovered, till thawed.
DEFROST 3½ to 5 minutes	Place loaf in a lightly greased 8x4x2-inch loaf dish. Cover with waxed paper. Cook till thawed, turning over once. Then raise and bake dough according to package directions.
DEFROST 15 to 20 seconds 20 to 30 seconds	Stack bread slices on a paper towel. Cook, uncovered, till thawed.
DEFROST 15 to 45 seconds	Place brownie or bar cookie on a plate. Cook, uncovered, till thawed.
DEFROST 1 to 2 minutes	Transfer cake from the foil pan to a plate. Cook, uncovered, till frosting on edges just begins to soften. (Watch carefully—frosting melts quickly.) Let stand, uncovered, 5 minutes or till thawed.
DEFROST 1 to 2 minutes	Place cake with its paper or plastic foam tray in the microwave oven. Cook, uncovered, till frosting on edges just begins to soften. (Watch carefully—frosting melts quickly.) Let stand about 8 minutes or till thawed.
DEFROST 1½ to 2½ minutes	Transfer cake from foil pan to a plate. Cook, uncovered, till thawed.
DEFROST 30 to 45 seconds 4 to 5 minutes	Transfer cheesecake from foil pan to a plate. Cook, uncovered, till edges are just soft and center is still icy, rotating plate a half-turn once. Let stand about 10 minutes or till thawed.
DEFROST 30 seconds to 1 minute 1 to 1½ minutes	Uncover container. Cook till softened.
DEFROST 1½ to 2 minutes	Open carton. Cook till partially thawed, shaking well once. Let stand about 10 minutes or till thawed, then shake well again before using.
HIGH 1½ to 2½ minutes	Place fruit in a small bowl. Cook, covered, till just thawed, stirring once.
HIGH 2½ to 3½ minutes	Remove one metal carton end, if present. Or, open carton. Place carton on a plate. Cook till partially thawed, breaking up fruit once. Break up fruit again, than let stand 5 minutes or till thawed.
HIGH 2½ to 3½ minutes	Cut a small slit in top of the pouch. Place pouch on a plate. Cook till partially thawed. Let stand about 5 minutes or till thawed.

Quick-Cooking Meats and Fish

For meals pronto, let your microwave oven lend a helping hand when it comes to cooking meats, poultry, and fish. In this chart you'll find a selection of fast-cooking cuts and pieces—choose one of these when time is running short.

Fish fillets cook more evenly in the microwave oven if you turn under any thin edges. This makes the fillets about the same thickness all over and the thinner ends won't be done before the thicker ends are.

Microwave-safe paper towels are perfect for cooking bacon. They prevent spattering by absorbing grease and moisture.

Also use paper towels for reheating breads so that the towels will absorb moisture and keep the bread surfaces dry. (See tip, page 18.)

Food & Amount

Meats
Bacon
  2 slices
  4 slices

Frankfurters
  1 frankfurter
  2 frankfurters

Ground meat *or* bulk sausages
  8 ounces
  1 pound

Ham, fully cooked boneless
  One 8-ounce boneless slice, cut ½ inch thick

Meatballs, 1-inch-round
  10 meatballs

Patties, ¾ inch thick
  One 4-ounce patty
  Two 4-ounce patties

Poultry
Chicken breast halves, boned and skinned, *or* turkey tenderloin steaks
  One 4-ounce piece
  Two 4-ounce pieces

Chicken breast halves with bone
  One 8-ounce half
  Two 8-ounce halves

Chicken drumsticks
  2 drumsticks
  6 drumsticks

Fish
Fish fillets *or* steaks
  8 ounces
  1 pound

Power Level & Time	Method
HIGH 2 to 3 minutes 3 to 4 minutes	Place bacon on a microwave-safe rack or paper plate. Cover with a paper towel. Cook till done, rotating rack or plate a half-turn once.
HIGH 30 seconds to 1½ minutes 1 to 2 minutes	Place frankfurters on a plate. Cover with waxed paper. Cook till heated.
HIGH 3½ to 5 minutes 6 to 7 minutes	Place loose ground meat or sausage in a casserole. Cook, covered, till no longer pink, stirring after every 2 minutes. Drain.
HIGH 5 to 6 minutes	Cut ham in half. Place pieces in a 1½-quart casserole. Cover with waxed paper. Cook till heated, turning ham pieces over once so outside edges face center of casserole.
HIGH 2 to 5 minutes	Place meatballs in a ring around edge of a plate. Cover with waxed paper. Cook till no longer pink, rotating plate a half-turn once.
HIGH 2 to 3 minutes 4½ to 7½ minutes	Place patties on a plate. Cover with waxed paper. Cook till no longer pink, turning patties over once so outside edges face center of plate and then rotating plate a half-turn.
HIGH 3 to 4 minutes 4½ to 5½ minutes	Place poultry in a baking dish. Cover with vented plastic wrap. Cook till no longer pink, turning pieces over once so outside edges face center of dish and then rotating dish a half-turn.
HIGH 7 to 9 minutes 12 to 14 minutes	Place chicken in a baking dish, skin side down. Cover with vented plastic wrap. Cook till no longer pink, turning pieces over once so outside edges face center of dish; rotate dish a half-turn.
HIGH 4 to 6 minutes 10 to 16 minutes	In a baking dish arrange drumsticks in a spoke fashion with meaty ends toward edges of dish. Cover with vented plastic wrap. Cook till no longer pink, turning drumsticks over once and then rotating dish a half-turn. (Remove each drumstick from dish when done.)
HIGH 2½ to 5 minutes 4 to 7 minutes	Place fish in a baking dish, turning under any thin edges so total thickness is the same. Cover with vented plastic wrap. For fillets: cook till fish flakes easily when tested with a fork, rotating dish a half-turn once. For steaks: cook till done, turning over once so outside edges face center of dish and then rotating dish a half-turn.

Heating Common Frozen Foods

A freezer plus a microwave oven equals quick and delicious dinners in a hurry. On this chart you'll find low-wattage microwave heating times for several frozen convenience foods.

Timings are for foods frozen in a refrigerator freezer. If you store your foods in a chest or upright freezer, expect the timings to be slightly longer.

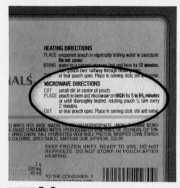

Microwave directions on many packaged foods are written for high-wattage ovens (600 to 700 watts). So when you're converting high-wattage timings to low-wattage timings, cook these foods for the time listed on the package. Then, if the food isn't heated, add 2 to 3 minutes more cooking time for every 5 minutes of original microwave-cooking time.

Food & Amount

Breads
Coffee cake
  1 serving-size wedge
  One 11½- to 13-ounce coffee cake

Dinner rolls
  1 roll
  2 rolls

Muffins
  1 muffin
  2 muffins

Pancakes, waffles, *or* French toast
  2 pieces
  4 pieces

Main Dishes
Burrito, beef
  One 5-ounce burrito

Casserole (meat, vegetable, and pasta combination)
  1 cup casserole
  2 cups casserole

Chicken, fried
  2 pieces
  4 pieces

Chicken, fried bite-size pieces
  6 pieces

Corn dogs
  1 corn dog
  2 corn dogs

Sandwiches, meat- and egg-filled biscuits
  1 4- to 4½-ounce sandwich
  2 4- to 4½-ounce sandwiches

Sausage links, brown and serve
  2 links
  4 links

Soup
  1 cup soup
  2 cups soup

Power Level & Time	Method
HIGH 1 to 1½ minutes 2 to 4 minutes	Transfer cake from foil pan to a plate. Cook, uncovered, till heated, rotating plate a half-turn once. Let stand, uncovered, till crumb topping is cool enough to eat.
HIGH 30 seconds to 1 minute 45 seconds to 1½ minutes	Place the dinner rolls on a paper towel. Cook, uncovered, till heated.
HIGH 30 to 45 seconds 45 seconds to 1 minute	Place on a plate or paper towel. Cook, uncovered, till heated. Let stand, uncovered, about 1 minute or till crumb topping is cool enough to eat.
HIGH 1 to 1½ minutes 2 to 3 minutes	Place the pancakes, waffles, or French toast on a plate in a single layer. Cook, uncovered, till breakfast item is heated.
HIGH 2 to 3½ minutes	Open ends of burrito package, then place on a plate. Cook till heated, rotating plate once.
HIGH 7 to 9 minutes 11 to 16 minutes	Transfer mixture to a casserole, if necessary. Cook, covered, till heated, stirring once.
HIGH 5 to 8 minutes 10 to 13 minutes	Place chicken on a paper plate or paper towel. Cook, uncovered, till heated, rotating plate or towel a half-turn once.
HIGH 2 to 3½ minutes	Place chicken on a paper plate. Cook, uncovered, till heated, turning over and rearranging once.
HIGH 1 to 1½ minutes 2 to 2½ minutes	Place corn dogs on a paper plate. Cook, uncovered, till heated, turning corn dogs over once and then rotating plate a half-turn.
HIGH 1 to 6 minutes* 1½ to 9 minutes*	Remove wrapper from sandwiches. Wrap sandwiches in paper towels. Cook till heated. *(For 1 sandwich: cook 1 to 2 minutes for a 4-ounce sandwich; 4 to 6 minutes for a 4½-ounce sandwich. For 2 sandwiches: cook 1½ to 2½ minutes for 4-ounce sandwiches; 6 to 9 minutes for 4½-ounce sandwiches.)
HIGH 45 seconds to 1½ minutes 1½ to 2 minutes	Place sausage links on a plate. Cover with waxed paper. Cook till heated.
HIGH 7 to 9 minutes 11 to 15 minutes	Transfer soup to a 1-quart casserole. Cook, covered, till heated, stirring once.

Heating Leftovers or Canned Foods

Need to quickly warm a dinner roll? Or, how about those leftover mashed potatoes? On this chart you'll find the timings to help you out. Listed are directions for heating a variety of foods that you might have left over in your refrigerator or stored on your kitchen shelves.

The timings are based on refrigerated temperature for leftovers, and room temperature for canned or packaged foods.

Just as in conventional cooking, the initial temperature of the food affects the microwave cooking time. That's why chilled leftover food will take longer to heat than canned food stored at room temperature.

Sugars and fats attract microwaves, so they heat faster than starches and proteins. Because of this you can expect the frosting on a sweet roll or cake (see charts, at right and page 68) to heat before the surrounding bread or cake.

Food & Amount

Breads
Dinner rolls
1 roll
2 rolls

Flour tortillas
1 tortilla
2 tortillas

French bread
½ of a 1-pound loaf

Sweet rolls
1 roll
2 rolls

Desserts
Pie, fruit
1 serving-size wedge

Ice cream topping
½ cup topping

Main Dishes
Beef stew
One 8½-ounce can
One 15-ounce can

Casserole (meat, vegetable, and pasta combination)
1 cup chilled casserole
2 cups chilled casserole

Chili
One 7½-ounce can
One 15-ounce can

Soup
1 cup chilled soup
2 cups chilled soup

Side Dishes
Potatoes, mashed
½ cup chilled potatoes
1 cup chilled potatoes

Rice, cooked
½ cup chilled rice
1 cup chilled rice

Vegetables
One 8- to 8½-ounce can
One 16-ounce can

Miscellaneous
Gravy *or* spaghetti sauce
1 cup canned *or* bottled gravy *or* sauce

Syrup, maple
½ cup syrup

Power Level & Time	Method
HIGH 15 to 20 seconds 20 to 30 seconds	Place the dinner rolls on a paper towel. Cook, uncovered, till heated.
HIGH 5 to 15 seconds 15 to 30 minutes	Place the flour tortillas between damp paper towels. Cook till heated.
HIGH 45 seconds to 1 minute	Wrap bread in a paper towel. Cook till heated.
HIGH 10 to 15 seconds 15 to 25 seconds	Place the sweet rolls on a paper towel. Cook, uncovered, till heated.
HIGH 30 to 45 seconds	Place pie on a plate. Cook, uncovered, till heated.
HIGH ½ to 1½ minutes*	Transfer topping to a 1-cup measure. Cook, uncovered, till heated. *(For chilled topping, cook for 1 to 2½ minutes or till heated.)
HIGH 3½ to 4½ minutes 4 to 6 minutes	Transfer the stew to a bowl. Cover with waxed paper. Cook till heated, stirring once.
HIGH 2 to 4 minutes 3 to 5 minutes	Transfer the casserole mixture to a casserole, if necessary. Cover with waxed paper. Cook till heated, stirring once.
HIGH 2 to 4 minutes 4 to 6 minutes	Transfer the chili to a bowl. Cover with waxed paper. Cook till heated, stirring once.
HIGH 4 to 6 minutes 7 to 9 minutes	Transfer 1 cup soup to a 2-cup measure; 2 cups soup to a 4-cup measure. Cook, uncovered, till heated, stirring once.
HIGH 1 to 3 minutes 3 to 5 minutes	Transfer potatoes to a bowl. Cover with waxed paper. Cook till heated. Gently stir before serving.
HIGH 1 to 1½ minutes 1½ to 2 minutes	Transfer the rice to a bowl. Cover with waxed paper. Cook till heated.
HIGH 2½ to 3½ minutes 4 to 5 minutes	Transfer *undrained* vegetable to a casserole. Cook, covered, till heated, stirring once. Drain.
HIGH 4 to 5 minutes	Transfer to a 2-cup measure. Cover with waxed paper. Cook till heated, stirring once.
HIGH 1 to 2½ minutes	Transfer the syrup to a 1-cup measure. Cook, uncovered, till heated.

Micro-Cooking Tips

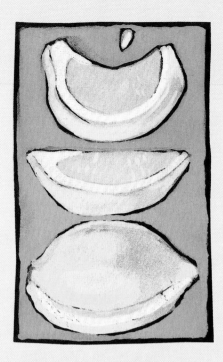

Crisping Snacks
Spread 1 cup stale or soft chips, crackers, or other snacks in a single layer on a plate. Cook, uncovered, on HIGH for 30 to 50 seconds. Let stand for 2 or 3 minutes. (Snacks will crisp as they stand.)

Making Plain Croutons
Spread 1 cup ½-inch bread cubes in a single layer on a plate. Cook, uncovered, on HIGH for 2½ to 3½ minutes or till dry, stirring after 2 minutes.

Making Quick Canapés
Arrange 7 to 9 bite-size bread pieces, toast pieces, or crackers on a plate lined with paper towels. Top with a desired spread, such as cream cheese, canned meat spread, or cheese spread. Cook, uncovered, on HIGH about 20 seconds or till the spread is heated.

Moistening Brown Sugar
In a 1-cup measure cook ½ cup water, uncovered, on HIGH for 2 to 5 minutes or till boiling.
Place ½ pound brown sugar in a container near water in oven. Cook, uncovered, on HIGH for 5 to 6 minutes or till softened. Immediately cover to store.

Cooking Onion
In a 1-cup measure cook chopped onion in 1 tablespoon margarine or butter, uncovered, on HIGH till tender. Allow 1½ to 2 minutes for ¼ cup onion and 2 to 3 minutes for ½ cup onion.

Peeling Tomatoes
In a 2-cup measure cook 1 cup water, uncovered, on HIGH for 3 to 6 minutes or till boiling. Holding a tomato on a fork, dip tomato in boiling water for 20 to 30 seconds. Then run cold water over tomato. Remove skin. (If peeling more than 2 tomatoes, bring *fresh* tap water to boiling. Do not reheat the used water. It will have lost oxygen in boiling, and may spray out of its container.)

Juicing Lemons
To soften lemons for easy juicing, halve 1 lemon. Place lemon in a bowl. Cook, uncovered, on HIGH for 30 to 45 seconds or till softened. Then squeeze out juice.

Plumping Dried Fruit
Place fruit in a 1-quart casserole. Add an equal amount of water. Cook, covered, on HIGH till boiling, stirring once. Allow 2 to 3 minutes for ½ cup dried currants or raisins; 4 to 5 minutes for ½ cup mixed dried fruit; 2 to 3 minutes for 1 cup dried apricots; and 4 to 5 minutes for 1 cup dried apples, currants,

raisins, figs, mixed fruit, peaches, or prunes. Let fruit stand for 5 to 10 minutes or till softened. Drain.

Warming Finger Towels

Soak 4 washcloths in water. Squeeze out excess water and roll each up. Place on a plate. Cook on HIGH for 2 to 3 minutes or till hot.

Hard-Cooked Egg

Carefully break an egg into a custard cup. Prick yolk and white each *3* times with a toothpick. Cover with vented plastic wrap. Cook on HIGH for 30 seconds to 1½ minutes or till done, rotating cup a quarter-turn after every 15 seconds. Let stand, covered, for 2 minutes. When cool, sieve, slice, or chop the cooked egg.

Melting Margarine

Place margarine or butter in a custard cup or bowl. Cook, un-covered, on HIGH till melted. Allow 45 seconds to 2 minutes for 2 table-spoons, 1½ to 2½ minutes for ¼ cup, and 1½ to 3 minutes for ½ cup margarine or butter.

Softening Margarine

Place margarine or butter in a bowl. Cook, uncovered, on HIGH till softened. Allow 10 to 15 seconds for ¼ cup and 15 to 25 seconds for ½ cup margarine or butter.

Softening Cream Cheese

Place unwrapped cream cheese in a bowl. Cook, uncovered, on HIGH till softened, rotating bowl a half-turn once. Allow 30 seconds to 1 minute for 3 ounces and 45 seconds to 1½ minutes for 8 ounces.

Melting Caramels

Place the unwrapped caramels in a bowl. Cook, uncovered, on HIGH till caramels become smooth when stirred, stirring after every minute. Allow 1 to 3 minutes for ½ of

a 14-ounce package (about 25 caramels) and 3 to 4 minutes for entire 14-ounce package of caramels.

Melting Chocolate

Place the unwrapped chocolate in a bowl. Cook, uncovered, on HIGH just till chocolate becomes smooth when stirred, stirring once.

Allow 1 to 2½ minutes for 1 ounce (1) square and 1½ to 5½ minutes for 2 ounces (2) squares; 1½ to 2½ minutes for 6 ounces (1 cup) pieces and 2 to 3 minutes for 12 ounces (2 cups) pieces.

Toasting Nuts

Place whole or chopped shelled nuts in a 2-cup measure. Cook, uncovered, on HIGH till toasted, stirring after every minute for the first 3 minutes, then after every 30 seconds during cooking.

Allow 2 to 4 minutes for ½ to 1 cup nuts. Whole shelled nuts may toast first on the inside, so open a few to check for doneness. At the first sign of toasting, spread whole or chopped nuts on a paper towel to cool. Let stand at least 15 minutes. (Nuts will continue to toast as they stand.)

Blanching Almonds

In a 2-cup measure cook 1 cup water, uncovered, on HIGH for 3 to 6 minutes or till boiling. Add ½ cup whole almonds. Then cook, uncovered, on HIGH for 1½ minutes. Drain, then rinse with cold water. When cool, slip off the almond skins.

Making Speedy Hot Chocolate

Pour ⅔ cup chocolate milk into a large mug. Cook, uncovered, on HIGH for 1½ to 6 minutes or till heated.

Cooking Pudding

In a 1-quart casserole combine pudding mix and milk. Cook, uncovered, on HIGH till boiling, stirring after every 2 minutes. Allow 7 to 11 minutes for one 4-serving-size package pudding mix in 2 cups milk, and 11 to 15 minutes for one 6-serving-size package in 3 cups milk. Cover and chill. (The pudding will thicken as it chills.)

Dissolving Unflavored Gelatin

In a bowl combine 1 envelope unflavored gelatin and ¼ cup water. Let stand for 5 minutes. Then cook, uncovered, on HIGH for 30 to 40 seconds or till dissolved.

Index

To add more great-tasting, low-wattage microwave recipes to your collection, turn to BETTER HOMES AND GARDENS® *Step-by-Step Microwave Cook Book.* In it you'll find dozens of reliable and practical recipes developed especially for your compact oven.